Acclaim for

How to Get Out of Your Own Way

"So heartfelt and inspirational it will likely leave readers with a new dedication to following their bliss." —*Publishers Weekly*

"The author was obviously born with wisdom many others aren't fortunate enough to possess...Part memoir, part life manual, an uplifting and inspirational guide to regaining control of your life." —*Kirkus Reviews*

"An inspirational read!...Gibson encourages readers with a revealing, self-reflecting journey." —*Upscale* Magazine

"A candid and honest tome, filled with Gibson's life experiences, interspersed with lessons learned and inspirational messages." —Examiner.com

"You will all love this book and will want to grab copies to give as gifts to your friends and family members. It's about time someone uses their position to inspire the masses." —Zimbio.com

"I've watched Tyrese for many years—I've watched him succeed; I've watched him fail; I've seen him as a beneficiary of serendipity; and I've watched him suffer at his own hand. And in the recent years, as we've become friends, I've witnessed Tyrese Gibson learn *how to get out of his own way* as he wrestled his destiny from the fickle hands of fate." —Will Smith

HOW TO GET OUT
OF YOUR OWN WAY

TYRESE
GIBSON

GRAND CENTRAL
PUBLISHING

NEW YORK   BOSTON

Grand Central Publishing
Hachette Book Group
237 Park Avenue
New York, NY 10017

www.HachetteBookGroup.com
Printed in the United States of America

Originally published in hardcover by Grand Central Publishing.

First Trade Edition: May 2012
10 9 8 7 6 5 4 3 2 1

Grand Central Publishing is a division of Hachette Book Group, Inc. The Grand Central Publishing name and logo is a trademark of Hachette Book Group, Inc.

The Hachette Speakers Bureau provides a wide range of authors for speaking events. To find out more, go to www.hachettespeakersbureau.com or call (866) 376-6591.

The publisher is not responsible for websites (or their content) that are not owned by the publisher.

The Library of Congress has cataloged the hardcover edition as follows:
Tyrese.
    How to get out of your own way / Tyrese Gibson. —1st ed.
    p. cm.
  ISBN 978-0-446-57222-4
    1. Tyrese. 2. Singers—United States—Biography. 3. Rap musicians—United States—Biography. 4. Motion picture actors and actresses—United States—Biography. I. Title.
  ML420.T976A3 2011
  782.421643092—dc22
  [B]

2010048159

ISBN 978-0-446-57223-1 (pbk.)

Contents

Author's Note

Thank you to all of my loved ones and fans from around the world who have supported everything I've done throughout my career, from the Coke commercial when I was sixteen to all of my different albums and films. It's also possible that someone referred you to this book and you've never heard of me a day in your life. If this is the first time you're getting to know me, I just hope you will be able to embrace me for who and what I am and the things that I stand for and the way I see my life. I'm going to take you on a little journey, from my childhood to where I am now. Hopefully you'll walk away being made aware of a few things and seeing relationships, love, and other perspectives just a little differently than the way you do now.

Although I won't be able to control how people respond to certain things that I write or reveal, my genuine intention is not to embarrass or throw anybody under the bus. I'm putting myself out there by writing about the many things I was exposed to, my actions, and the choices I made. Although I can't stop people from feeling a certain way, you all need to know that I'm not coming from an angry or spiteful place. I'm just speaking my truth.

Some of the conversations in this book were taken from memory and, in those instances, have been paraphrased.

I want to say thank you now for picking up this book and being willing to take this journey with me. I hope you enjoy it.

—Tyrese, December 2010

A Prayer Before We Begin

Before I do anything of significance in my life, I always start it off with a prayer, and that's not going to change with my first book. So please join me in this prayer, wherever you are...

Father God, I just want to say thank You for everything that You are, and everything You've always been to me. There are a lot of people with eyes who still can't see, so I thank You for allowing me to see what's around me. Thank You for clarity and for building bridges of understanding in my life. Before I sit and eat to nourish my body, my grace and prayer is to You, to thank You for allowing me to eat what I want, when I want, where I want, and with whom I want, because I know there are a lot of people around the world who don't have that as an option. I'm grateful for the opportunity to wake up and go out and be a living example of Your favor. I thank You for what You decided to bless *me* with. Father God, I wish I had a thousand tongues to thank You, because I'm alive, and I know You're not done with me yet. I am so grateful for the opportunity to use my influence to impact others. I surrender to Your will. Please bless the Love Circle and the people in my life so that they will find more strength in the rest of their days and weeks. Protect them, Father God.

Father God, I hope that people reading this book do not view anything within it as me showing off, gloating, or splashing my blessings in their face. I hope they look upon me as an example of someone with pure focus, determination, and execution, who literally started from the bottom in the ghetto streets of Watts. It was there that I decided I was tired of being tired, of worrying about my safety and my environment and that I wanted better for me and my family. It's only by Your grace and favor that I'm still here.

Father God, I pray that when my friends, family, loved ones, fans, and people who may have never even heard of me in their life read this book, they consider new possibilities. I pray that they don't allow their own mental blocks and upbringing to get in the way of new ideas. Most people around the world, including myself, are unknowingly suffering from self-sabotage and self-defeat and are literally blocking their *own* blessings. I pray that from the reading of this book they decide to join me on this lifelong journey of trying to master the art of getting out of their own way.

Prayer for the Love Circle

As you read this book, I pray that you are open to peeling back the many layers that have caused a blockage of your own blessings—blessings that will free you from being bound in self-destruction, self-sabotage, fear, doubt, and all the troubles that have caused you to live as the victim of your choices instead of living victoriously. I wrote this book to challenge your comfort zone and get you to consider that you might be living with your blinders on and forcing yourself to *not* see what you ordered for your own life. My extreme hope is to break through those thick walls of complacency and empower you to face your fears of the unknown.

Hopefully this book challenges you to see things outside of the bubble of reality you have created for yourself, and that you decide, like I have, to take that leap of faith, knowing that with God all things are possible and that you will land on your feet.

I pray that you stop yourself from wallowing in darkness and decide today to pull yourself into the light. You are *stronger* than you could ever know. I believe in you and I am rooting for you.

Trust in God to heal, provide, restore, and transform you. Know that there is power in making a choice. Choose today to be the unique design that you and only you were created to be. Be *bold* in your choices. Know that you can do any and everything through God who gives you strength (Philippians 4:13). Remember that today is a *new* day and that the past is just that—the *past*.

I don't believe in accidents. There is a *reason* you picked up this book. So stand tall, for your journey has led you here, to self-discovery, healing, and *victory*, and to a better place that will reveal a better you—the *real* you. I am already rejoicing and celebrating your liberation from the spiritual chains and bondage of your old habits, thoughts, and choices.

Thank You. Amen.

Okay, ladies and gents—breathe! I know that was a lot to process...

Now, mates, shall we begin this journey?

Foreword

I want to dedicate this book to a friend of mine, Sameer. Sameer lived in Dubai, but we met a few years ago at a party in Beverly Hills that was hosted by Donald Trump, who was giving a presentation about his plans in Dubai. Sameer and I had fun partying and found that we shared a lot of the same views. We became friends and were brainstorming a few possible business ventures, so we stayed in touch. He started telling me all his plans, what he wanted to do with his life, and I was letting him in on all my plans. I took him to my office and introduced him to people I worked with, and he was impressed that I had accomplished so much at such a young age. He was just very inspirational and motivational to me, a really good guy.

One of the things I mentioned to him was that I wanted to write this book. At the time, the title I had in mind was just *Get Out of Your Own Way*. He thought it was a great idea and was extremely positive about the project. After that, Sameer left the country to go close some deals in Dubai, and I didn't see him for about six months. Then he showed up in LA for my twenty-ninth birthday, and he had something in his hand, a gift for me. He just said, "Here," and put a book in my lap. I looked at the cover and in bold letters it said *How to Get Out of Your Own Way*. I noticed that he had added the words "How to" in front of "Get Out of Your Own Way." It was a mock-up of my book cover, with only the title on it, but it looked like he had it made at a print shop and it had a little picture of me on the spine of the book, which I had never seen before. On the back he had put a few inspirational quotes from his favorite authors. I opened the book, and inside, the pages were all blank. I sat there with the book in my lap, flipping through the empty pages. He told me, "The rest is on you. Write the book."

Now, at this point, I still hadn't started writing or compiling any text for the book. I didn't know what the process was going to be, but all of a sudden I felt pressured to make the book a reality. I had this blank book in my hands and I couldn't ignore it. Sameer had planted the seed and now I really had to put some *words* onto those empty pages.

That night Sameer, our crew, and I went to a club and it was insane—we had a blast. Soon after, he went back overseas for work. And then some stuff went down that I don't fully understand.

Sameer's sister called me, flipping out, and told me that he was in deep trouble. He didn't want me to know, but he had been in jail for three months and they had tried to get him out but it didn't look like that would happen. She told me it had to do with his business, that many people in the company he worked for had been arrested.

Trying to be a good friend and supporter, I prayed with him. I tried my best to encourage and motivate him every time we talked. He was totally depressed, sad, and miserable because he didn't have a court date and wasn't sure when he would ever get out. The entire time, I was thinking to myself that I have never felt like I was in jail as much as I did from talking to him while he was in jail. Because we both love life, our freedom, partying, and hanging out, and he went nuts in there. I knew he was having suicidal thoughts, and every time we talked, I gave him all the good energy I could. When it seemed like he was almost at his breaking point I sent him the first draft of my manuscript for the book to try and keep his spirits up. When he finished reading the pages, he told me they had inspired and motivated him to hold on and not give up.

Sameer ended up spending a whole year in jail. When he was finally released, he had a pending court date but he was all fired up. When he called me he was back to his old self. His energy and positive spirit were screaming through the phone. He was looking forward to enjoying his life and picking up the pieces.

A few months later, when I was in the middle of working on the manuscript, I got a phone call from his sister, who told me that Sameer had jumped from a high-rise building in Dubai and killed himself.

I was at a loss for words. One of the first things I thought when I found out about his death was how crazy it was, because at thirty-one years old I had never known anyone who had committed suicide. I didn't know how to process something I had never experienced before. I started thinking about how Sameer had already done a year in prison, and even though it was rough and he didn't think he could make it, he *had* made it. Why would anybody get out of prison and decide to take their own life, not even a month after getting released? I was conflicted because ultimately he had pushed me to write the book I was now calling *How to Get Out of Your Own Way*. He had made an impact on it by changing the title, but he ended up getting in *his* own way and taking his own life.

If you don't figure out your life and get out of your own way, your choices could possibly lead to a life of misery, bad circumstances, and as you can see, something as extreme as suicide.

I want all my readers to know that this book is coming from a real place. It's not just me sitting down, deciding to put a bunch of words together so I can pat myself on the back and say "Hey, I wrote a book." Hopefully the information and true experiences that I speak on here can get *in* the way of somebody else deciding that life's pressures are too tough and prevent them from staying in dysfunctional or bad situations or ultimately taking their own life.

I do know that my words and prayers and our conversations helped Sameer for some time. He told me that my book had really inspired and impacted him to keep fighting. I can't help but think that there were some other dynamics and forces within him or around him, beyond what I knew, that made him end his life. A few months after he died, we found out that he was exonerated and all the charges against him were dropped.

Despite this tragic story, I don't want to start this book on a sad note, because what Sameer did for me and what I will truly remember him for was that he really pushed me to get the words on the blank pages. I had mentioned to him that I wanted to write a book and he really helped me follow through with it.

Although I wasn't sure I could sit down and write a whole book, I realized that I was actually sitting on a gold mine of inspirational concepts. Unknowingly, I had started the process of creating material for this book several years before, when I decided to share more about my life with my fans through voicemail and online messages on Twitter, MySpace, Facebook, and a few blogs. At first I thought I would just talk about my new music and movies, but the interaction grew into something much more personal, more real and genuine than I ever could have imagined. On my voicemail service, when people leave a message, I'm not the only person who can hear it. Anyone on the service can listen. As I began to share more about what I was thinking and what was going on in my life, people who heard my messages told me they appreciated what I was saying and began to leave their own confessions and testimonies. We were hearing each other's strength and giving each other the permission to do better and want better, to take the steps to change. That's why I dubbed this community the Love Circle.

Over the last decade, I have come to realize that God's purpose for me is to reach out to people. I leave the voicemail messages and I tweet—and now I'm writing this book—because I want to give people permission to want better for themselves and take their lives to another level, and sometimes we just need information on how to get it done. When I was younger, I was determined to get out of Watts and become a singer. All we wanted to do as young kids in the hood was to get ahold of somebody who was already in the music game to help us figure it out. I have always been curious about life. Ever since I was young I've been asking questions to find out what things mean, but it wasn't part of my conscious personal strategy to improve; I just wanted and needed to *know*. I was lucky to find a few people along the way who gave me information to help me on my journey. I'm dying to put that same energy out there, to give someone the same permission that these people gave me.

I have found that a conversation with somebody who drops some heavy stuff on you can make you look at yourself and your life a little differently. You can still be very in tune with yourself and your purpose and the things that you stand for, but you can become a person who can reach for something better. And so all these important conversations became part of an ongoing mission for me to take a piece of knowledge, a piece of information, a different perspective or outlook and add them to my life. I've been picking up life's building blocks along the way, and *rebuilding myself* with a block from each person.

I am now passing these real-life experiences along because honestly, I would feel guilty knowing the things I know and not be willing to speak on it. As a child of God I feel a certain responsibility to share the many things I know and have been exposed to. It would be unfair to a little boy who is hungry like I was, who doesn't know how to figure out his life. I would feel guilty about knowing what I know now and keeping it to myself because my loyal supporters and fans from the beginning have my back. If they didn't support my albums, movies, and other passion projects, then my career probably would have faded out a long time ago. Since I can't go and actually pay everyone back individually for helping me live an amazing life and lifestyle, I can send out the knowledge and information I've got and hope it makes a difference.

I'm not claiming to be God or Jesus, nor will I ever attempt to be. I'm just trying to get others to realize their power and spirit. Every message I leave comes from my heart. As much as the voicemail messages do for people, at this point I believe they're doing more for me, because I'm able to express myself knowing that there are a lot of people listening who could be impacted by what I say. It does a lot for me to know I'm helping in some way.

As the Love Circle grew I felt more of a responsibility to think about what I was saying and what my actions were along with it, because people were really paying attention to me now. Even though I had been famous for a few years before I started leaving the voicemail messages, I still wasn't used to the idea of fame, and I'd never had the chance to get to know my fans on such an intimate level. At a concert, fans don't usually get to talk to the performers, and if you do meet, it's always quick. I never had the chance to sit down and have a full-on conversation. But with the Love Circle I'm able to get to know the people who support me—not only as fans but on different levels. I try to nurture and educate and make people aware of things that they never knew or thought about, or were never made aware of—not even by their own fathers, mothers, uncles, brothers, or grandparents.

Over the past few years, I've gone through some momentous life changes that have given me a completely new outlook on life, and I'll talk about some of those changes here. All the problems I had have affected me personally, professionally, and spiritually, and are issues I've been dealing with for quite some time. I've felt a lot of pain in my life, and I know just about every form it can take. I have to admit that while writing this I've felt very vulnerable and exposed, because anybody who knows me knows I'm a very private person living a very public life. It's on my heart to share my perspective and outlook in the hope that it might bring some level of clarity and understanding about how to get through different challenges and help others make better choices so that they won't go down the long road and bump their heads the way I did.

What I've done is organize the book into a series of questions. The reason for this is that these are the basic, fundamental questions that helped me redefine who I was as a human being and evolve into a new man. I want to emphasize that these are my opinions, and this is my story. I've learned that experience is your *highest* truth and only you can define your own truth. Don't let anyone tell you differently. I'm just here to provide you with my personal road map that helped me understand myself better. I've learned over the years from talking to many people of all backgrounds—from ghettos and middle America, whites, blacks, and in between—that most people have goals and missions and places they want to take their lives personally and professionally. But most don't have a sense of direction. I've realized that hopes, dreams, and ambition without a clear sense of direction will leave you feeling *stuck* in your hopes and dreams. So I pray that something in this book will give you a better sense of direction to help you *achieve* your hopes and dreams.

I'm not here to say that everything you think and do is

wrong, and that I'm Mr. Perfect. As you will see, I am anything but perfect. I continue to learn new things every day. They say you can't teach an old dog new tricks; I don't believe that. I believe that the best thing you can ever do for yourself is allow your spirit to stay open to all possibilities and try to consider new things without limiting yourself to only what *you* know and are comfortable with. Your life should be an ongoing and growing process.

Now that you are reading this book I want to officially welcome you to the Love Circle. With all that out of the way, let's get it started, shall we?

A Message to Our Youth

I'm well aware of my influence now and I don't take it lightly. I want you to really listen to what I'm about to say. This is not just another book. I'm going to try and make you aware of things that are around the corner long before you get there. I want you to trust and believe that I know what I'm talking about. I don't know it all, but what I do know, I'm sharing with you. I'm hoping to make you aware of things that your father, your big brother, or even your mother may not have told you.

Throughout this book I'll be sharing some stories about how I became the master of my environment. Even if you're a teenager you can be the master of your environment and the master of your own future, and I want that for you. Everything in your life should be about moving forward and progressing toward what you imagine for yourself. So if you don't like your environment, change it. If you don't like your circumstances, change them. Do whatever you have to do to create a better mind-set for yourself.

Part of that is worrying about yourself—or rather, *focusing* on yourself. Sometimes we get so focused on other people, like a boyfriend or girlfriend, that we can't see ourselves clearly. I want you to concentrate on your *own* goals before thinking about someone else's. Dropping out is not an option, so you have to stay focused on school, and if your friends are leading you down the wrong path, surround yourself with a better circle of friends.

When I was younger, I wanted better for myself. I worked my butt off and went to high school early every day and graduated in three years. It wasn't that I was without pressures. I had to grow up quickly and most likely you do, too. I knew early on, when I was eight or nine, that people around me were selling drugs and I saw the lifestyle the drug dealers had, compared to mine. I was poor and hungry and they had nice cars, brand-new shoes, and T-shirts. They were living in a nice spot with furniture, and I knew that all those things didn't come from having a regular job. Everybody in the hood knew that money came from dudes slinging dope, weed, and sherm.

Now, people weren't trying to pressure me or talk me into selling crack or weed. I don't remember any of my boys saying *Yo, you wanna get some money? You need to come do this!* No one said that to me, but being exposed to all that stuff was still peer pressure. Seeing images like those, when you're in the situation I was, can make any man or adolescent decide they want to mess with that so they can get money while they're in high school. They want and need money to buy a car, some nice clothes so they can impress the girls at school, or just want to have money for lunch or a bus token, instead of being out there hungry and broke.

But I remember purposely deciding that even though all

that stuff *looked* cool, even though I had seen tons of money counted in front of me and the financial benefits of selling drugs and weed, I also knew that some of my boys were going to jail and a lot of dudes in my neighborhood were having their houses raided for drug money. Something in my mind told me to stay away from it.

Don't get caught up in all your friends' stuff. If all your friends are having sex, don't think you have to! I know the media—videos, magazines, music, movies, television—make sex seem cool and easy, your friends at school are talking about it, and you want to fit in and do it, too. But there's no need to try and live up to all the images around you. There will be plenty of time to have sex, and plenty of time to get into a relationship. The more you know yourself, the better you'll be at making decisions about whom you'll want to be with. I know you may get lonely sometimes, but being alone is nothing to be afraid of. Learn to enjoy and embrace who you are and get to know yourself in the process.

When I was younger I didn't get with a lot of girls. Not that I didn't want to, but I see now that may have saved me. Several of my homeys and both my sisters had kids when they were still in high school. I witnessed with my own eyes how having babies made their lives more difficult. Their lives stopped, they couldn't hang out, they couldn't afford a babysitter because they were broke; they just got bogged down with the responsibility of raising a child. Whether the pregnancies were accidental or something these kids decided to do, they tried their best, but some of them in today's words would be considered "deadbeat parents" because they dumped their kids on their mothers, fathers, or even random neighbors so that they could still go clubbing, hang out, and be young.

A lot of young guys are ready to make it happen, but they don't have to worry about the same things as young women. The consequences are not the same. I know it can be tough for teenagers to do what someone my age is asking them to do, and ignoring your elders is what being a teenager is all about, right? But you should know that movies and TV don't tell you the whole story, and someone in my position needs to keep it all the way real with you. There are too many girls in junior high and high school who are getting pregnant when they don't even know anything about life or about themselves. Do you want "teen mom" or "teen dad" to be your story? I hope not. I had my first child when I was twenty-eight—when I was ready. At that point, the only thing I didn't have in my life was a child, and it was the right time. A child shouldn't be the thing that makes you start to grow up. If you're young and are already having sex, stop! There are too many young guys out there making babies and you have to know that that doesn't have to be your life.

A young boy doesn't have a clue how to be a father, and a young girl has no idea how to be a mother. Why? Because they're *kids*. You may have been exposed to a lot and some of you may have raised yourself and that can make you feel mature and much older in spirit, but you're young—period. So stop there and don't convince yourself otherwise. I'll never forget a conversation I had with a sixteen-year-old mother of two who told me why she was motivated to have children. She couldn't keep a boyfriend, her parents had basically abandoned her, and she had nothing in her life that was consistent. She told me that whether she stayed with the baby daddy or not, her babies would never leave her side.

But think about it: Have you ever seen a movie, a documentary, or anything on television where you see a teenager who has a kid and they're happy? The reality is, these kids with kids are just stuck—at home, watching and caring and worrying about their child. It's not that they don't love their babies, but their futures are altered.

You may have career goals and all kinds of plans that you are putting together, but with a child it won't be about you anymore. Your decisions and your plans will always have to include that child. Every day. Do you really think your mother or father will feel like raising another child when they've already raised you? If you don't have a father, mother, or grandparents, you'll have to do it on your own. Are you really ready for a twenty-four-hour-a-day-seven-day-a-week baby?

And here's a harsh reality, ladies: More than likely this boy you decided to have sex with will be too young to be a father. Ask any single mother to tell you stories about how much shit she went through when she was pregnant, how she worries about money, and how she struggles to get the little youngsta—the baby daddy—to step up to the plate and do his part. You don't want to deal with any of that at your age. You want to hang out, you want to stay in school and *not* drop out because you can't bring your child to school with you. You want to have fun, you want to go to the mall, you want to be *young*. So be smart, be real smart, and stay far away from that madness!

Focus on your future and your goals and become whatever it is you imagine for yourself. Then, when you can hold yourself down and are in control of your life, you can make the choice to accept a partner and bring a new life into the world.

If for whatever reason you end up having sex—let's be real—you make sure to have that kid you're having sex with put on a condom. Be the master of your environment and stay in control. Don't *occasionally* have sex without a condom, because all it takes is *one* sexual moment that can create a child, and that very child will be with you for a lifetime, whether the boy you decided to have sex with is with you or not.

Let's be very clear, young ladies: There are a lot of older guys out there who get their kicks by sleeping with girls who are under eighteen. I want you to know that any man who is trying to have sex with an underage girl is a criminal—period, end of story. Some girls in junior high or high school are attracted to older guys because they claim that the guys in their schools are immature. I understand, because I was in high school and I remember girls saying that exact thing. But understand this: For whatever reason you may decide to become sexually active with an older man, you have to know these men are committing a crime. Because they're older, they know more than you and they are able to manipulate your mind and emotions to get you to see things the way they want you to see them. I'm disgusted with older guys who want girls your age because you're vulnerable and they take advantage of what you don't know. They want to have sex with you and make you believe that they love you. Know yourself, get in control of your life, and do not let some older man come into your life and mess it all up. Just because you're younger, doesn't mean you can't control your environment, your actions, or who comes into your life.

And for the young guys out there: If you don't have a father, start spending time with your friends' fathers, or figure out who your favorite male teacher is, and ask him a lot of questions about life, about issues, situations, problems, or feelings—any thoughts you may have. Don't be embarrassed to ask questions. Don't be afraid to say what's on your mind. There is no such thing as a dumb question. What may be dumb to you might actually give you clarity and closure on something that has been bouncing around in your head for a long time. I was lucky to find mentors around me, even though my dad wasn't there. Those guys saved my life. I hope there is at least one person out there who can do the same for you. If I just so happen to be that one person, keep reading because I've got a lot to share with you.

Chapter 1

Child-Hood

When I first met my mentor John Bryant, he told me, *Most of who we are as adults is somehow directly connected to our childhood.* I had to really sit with that one for a while and see if it was true for me. After I pondered on this and started making those connections, what I discovered blew me away. A lot of who I am—my habits, relationships, likes, dislikes, and motivations, the things I stand for and the way I see this world—are all connected to my childhood. Once I decided that I no longer wanted to carry those childhood burdens, my journey to get out of my own way began. They say that ignorance is bliss, but the clarity from knowing what I know has changed my life. I connected the burdens I was carrying to my childhood memories and vowed to disown it and let it all go.

I can remember always thinking and imagining my life beyond where I was. I can remember sitting on the front porch in the hood at night looking at the stars and letting my thoughts run wild. Never did I once see or imagine being a star in any form of show business. I remember once thinking to myself that if there really was a God and he was hearing all the prayers from us throughout the hood, I hoped he'd somehow hear mine. Even back then something in me believed that there was a better life somewhere out there—I guess watching *Lifestyles of the Rich and Famous* played a small part in that thinking. I just had no clue how I was going find it or where to start.

Throughout my childhood I was exposed to the most

extreme levels of self-love and self-hate. I lived and witnessed it all—killings, gang violence, drive-by shootings, domestic abuse, drug and alcohol abuse, crack cocaine, heroin addicts using needles, prostitution, teen pregnancy, love, encouragement, sports, talent shows, good and bad teachers, hunger, poverty. It was a harsh reality. When I grew into my early teens, a wise man told me, *Son, every lesson is a blessing but you will* grow *through what you* go *through.* And boy did I go through some shit!

A few months ago, I went back to the park in Watts where I first performed in public. I was back in my old hood at a memorial service for Tommy Jacquette, who had started the Watts Summer Festival. He had been the backbone of the community and my high school music teacher, Reggie Andrews, and Congresswoman Maxine Waters had asked me to be there and say a few words. I didn't say no because I had reaped the benefits from what Mr. Jacquette had brought to the community. And so I went back to the park—to the exact same basketball gym and stage where I first performed at a Head Start Talent Show when I was fourteen. I didn't get famous from that first public performance, but I did win, and that gave me the confidence to continue with my singing when my family had told me to shut up for being too loud around the house.

At the memorial, I went onstage and started talking at the podium. I told the audience how people like myself were able to reap the benefits from the peace and harmony that Mr. Jacquette had tried his best to bring to the community. And then I said, "You know, I remember when…" and as I said those words I looked to my left and actually saw my younger self, next to me, like a vision. I hadn't been on that stage in seventeen years. I'm taller now, so I was looking down at my old self, standing there, not moving, because I never moved when I sang at that first show. Back then I had been nervous as hell, so I just stood in one place and held my microphone while I sang. As I imagined my younger self standing there, so much was running through my mind: Look how much I've seen around the world. Look how much I've done, look how many places I've been, how many amazing people I've met, all of the movies I've been in and the albums I put out, the road and the tours I've been on, and it all started standing in *this one place*, right here. I started crying. I was a grown man having a meltdown in front of everybody. And when I finally got myself together, I thanked Reggie Andrews and Don Lee, the first person who had allowed me to be in that first talent show. I said, "I want to thank you for giving me permission to be great. You believed in me and I've been around the world and I've seen the greatest that life has to offer, and it all started right here, standing in this exact spot." I was standing on the same stage but I was a different man—different than that fourteen-year-old Tyrese could have imagined. I don't live in the hood now, but I'll always be from the hood and I will never ever, ever not remember what I've been through. My journey and my perspective and what I was exposed to keep me real.

My mother and father are from St. Louis, Missouri, the city where I was conceived as the youngest of four children.

My oldest sister has a different father, and my second sister and my older brother have the same mother and father as me. Since then, my father had another son and daughter.

My father is a singer, but he never really got anything off the ground. He's a wanderer and a dreamer, an artist always searching for his next break. One day, he decided that his dream would come true in Los Angeles, so he moved the family out west. A few months after they arrived I was born in a city called Watts in South Central Los Angeles, at Martin Luther King, Jr. General Hospital.

My mother always told me that I was a hyper kid. Looking back, I think it's because we moved around so much and never really settled down in one place, but it's just the way I am.

When I was really young, we lived in an area south of Watts near Washington Boulevard, a bit removed from the real nitty-gritty of South Central, Compton, and Watts. Money was tight, and my dad wasn't there most of the time. He seemed to be gone more than he was there and I was too young to understand why he would stay with us for weeks at a time and then disappear. He would come back every so often, but even when he was there, before he left for good, I witnessed a lot of what no kid should be exposed to.

When my brother and sisters and I were supposed to be asleep we could hear my mother and father physically fighting in their room, calling each other every name in the book. Being exposed to the friction and negative energy of their relationship is how what I considered "love" started to take its effect on me. One would assume that because we were young what they were doing didn't impact us, but it did in a major way. Hearing and seeing my dad treating my mother like nothing, cursing her out, and beating her whenever the moment presented itself, made me believe that's what love was. At some point their marriage came to a halt and my mother seemed lost and alone. Pops would come around here and there, but we all pretty much knew it was over between my mother and father.

It was during this time that I feel like my mother's love for me and our whole family was the strongest. She was beautiful, and still is, in my eyes. If you want to know where I got my smile, look no farther than my mama. She kept her long, flowing hair in French braids that made her look youthful, energetic, and alive.

Mama would take us to church three to four days a week for services and choir practice. It was a safe haven and I was getting to know God, who was getting to know me. I loved the energy of being around a lot of people because it gave me another stage to crack jokes and do my thing. I would play around and was often too hyper during services when I was really young, because I'd usually get bored just sitting there.

Mama worked as a waitress at Jordan's Café and Stops Drive-In, which was on Imperial and Central, but has since been torn down. She used to bring us leftover food and that was like Thanksgiving for us kids. But with all of the mouths to feed we were still broker than broke so the county helped us out with some money. We received social security, food stamps, and county checks, and started getting WIC vouchers when I was in elementary school, after my oldest sister had her first child. A couple years later, when I was in junior high, my other sister had a kid, so we qualified for more. Even back then, I remember thinking, *Where is the money going?* We had food in the house but there were so many of us—Moms, Pops, my sisters, their kids, my brother and me—that the food would come in and disappear almost as fast. You can't think that the cereal is going to be there tomorrow so you've got to eat five or six bowls in a row to get your share. When I think back on my childhood, there were very few memories that aren't accompanied by an overwhelming sense of hunger. We were hungry all the time.

Mornings at my house were real quiet, and some of the best mornings were when we had cereal or oatmeal, or if we were really lucky, Cream of Wheat. When I was a youngsta I used to love eating my cereal, when we had it, and watching cartoons like *Tom & Jerry*, *Thundercats*, *Transformers*, *He-Man*, *Heathcliff*, *Duck Tales*, and *Inspector Gadget*. I also loved playing video games on the Atari 2600, ColecoVision, and original Nintendo that we got as hand-me-downs from neighbors; Super Mario Brothers, Mike Tyson's Punch-Out!, and Tecmo Bowl were my favorites. But most mornings we didn't have any food, so I was motivated to go to school because that was where I could escape the madness at my house and get meal tickets. Some days, if I didn't go to school, I didn't eat.

Gangs were all around us in that part of the hood, but there were also a lot of good people with incredible hearts, who beyond what money they did or didn't have would do damn near anything for you. The everyday mission of most good people who live in the hood and who don't have a bad bone in their bodies was to stay safe, to protect and take care of their kids and their families, to get to and from work or school and stay out of harm's way, and to pray that none of those stray bullets meant for someone else would end up in them.

There were a lot of different personalities in the hood throughout all the different neighborhoods I lived in, and back then we used to talk about people who seemed like they did the same thing day after day. I remember way back when I was around six or seven there was a lady named Miss Jameson who was friends with my mother who would sit on her front porch. For what seemed like ten hours a day she would just sit there and peel her beans. Everyone loved Miss Jameson. In Watts there was a super old lady who lived directly across from us on 113th and Grape who would literally call the police if anyone stepped on her grass. Most of the people in the hood had guns and were very capable of hurting this old woman, but she was more gangsta than all of us. Directly around the corner there was the blind man who would give us a few pennies to run to the store for him because his heavy-set wife refused to do it anymore. I once asked my brother, "Why would a man be with a woman he can't see? And why would a woman be with a man who is blind?"

He would just shake his head and laugh. It's funny that when I look back on my life I remember never being afraid to ask questions about things I didn't understand.

There was also my mother's best friend, Blanche. I believe she was part Latina and part white but she had the soul of a black woman because she grew up in the hood. Blanche lived across the street from a burger stand called Lee's that we went to all the time. Her beautiful daughters were always outside on the porch or in their front yard looking so pretty. If I had the courage to ask them out, I probably would have taken them to Lee's. My whole family loved Lee because he let my mother keep a running tab that had to be paid at the end of the month. That didn't last too long because she was always late in paying.

After my moms and pops broke up for good, my mother met another man who tried to do right by her, and by us. We called him Mr. Charlie and he became my stepfather. Mr. Charlie was much older than Mama—he was retired—but he was exactly what we needed in our lives at that point. He was a good man and taught us a lot. I can honestly say that a lot of who I am as a man came from Mr. Charlie, and for that I will always love and thank him.

Charlie was definitely a neat freak and was always very strict about making sure we kept things clean and organized. Whenever he had us clean up, he would tell us to get on our hands and knees on the carpet and pick up any piece of lint or dirt in the rug and put it in a trash bag that we carried with us. He had this old, antique leather furniture that was nicer than anything I had ever seen before. Everything in the house was dusted and polished at all times, which was so different from what we were used to, because before Mr. Charlie moved in with us we were just plain filthy. At the time, it seemed tedious and unnecessary, but Mr. Charlie made sure I always paid attention to the tiniest of details, and it's a habit I've carried into to adulthood. He brought a much-needed sense of structure, discipline, and responsibility that we had been lacking.

We moved with Mr. Charlie to 113th and Grape, in Watts, where I met Daniel, a Latino kid who lived in the corner house right next to the projects. His house backed up on a big field filled with trash that people would just dump there to rot.

There was also a huge broken-down truck and the shell of a camper that was getting rustier by the day. Daniel became one of my best childhood homeys. We would find three or four unwanted old piss-stained mattresses in the field, line them up back-to-back, and do gymnastic flips for hours and hours. To us, those mattresses were as good as any piece of real gym equipment.

Daniel, his brother, my brother, and I would run around his house and the field playing cops and robbers for four or five hours every day. My brother had a big-looking "gun," which was really just part of a broken car jack. My weapon was not as elaborate, just a piece of wood that I found on the ground. Daniel and I would run through the backyard and into the field to get away from him. Someone would yell, "Okay, go!" and then it was a free-for-all. "I shot you first. No, I shot you first!" The truth is, we loved Daniel's backyard and that field because we could just run free for hours playing our childhood games. It was the only chance we got to escape from the realities of our lives and the world around us. It's funny to think about those times, because despite being poor and hungry, we were too innocent to realize how bad things were around us. To us, that was just life. We made the best of it, enjoying the good, and trying not to think about the bad.

Mr. Charlie was strict, but we were lucky enough to have him in our lives for several years until he passed away. I had never experienced death before, and it hit me hard, real hard. I vividly remember seeing him resting in his casket at the funeral, and touching his hands one last time, as they lay folded across his chest. The coldness of his skin sent a chill through my body that was unlike anything I had ever felt before. It's one thing when you lose a childhood homey or hear that someone in the neighborhood got killed, and it's another thing to lose someone you lived and communicated with every day, who watched television with you every night, and whose voice you can still hear ringing in your ears. I remember thinking while I was crying, *When are you gonna get up, Mr. Charlie?* Then turning to God I asked, *This isn't real, right? He's not really gone, right? What am I supposed to do now? Who's gonna teach me the things I need to know about life?* I didn't get any answers, so I just kept crying and missing him. I used to dream about Mr. Charlie a lot after he first died. We lived in that same house for several years afterward.

After he was gone for a while, I realized that Mr. Charlie had been a stabilizing influence that held our family together, and once he died, something happened that I've never quite been able to pin down. I think the years of dysfunction between my mother and father finally came to a boil, and took my mama over the edge. As a result, she turned to the bottle. She started drinking, and once she got going, she didn't stop for twenty-seven years.

I was a hyperactive kid, and I'm not exaggerating. I was the funniest little dude you'd ever be around. I was just way over the top. Everything was on ten. People used to say, *As soon as he wakes up he's gonna be out of here, from the morning on, until he comes back here to take his ass to sleep.* And that was the story of my life. People who knew me knew I was the kid who was hyper, funny, loud. I made it a point that everybody around me had a good time. But I had no idea when to stop. I was diagnosed with ADHD and they gave me some Ritalin to calm me down, but that stuff didn't quite work on me. I didn't have the radar that told me when to quit. I got kicked out of Grape Street Elementary School because of it, and was sent to what they call a "behavioral private school."

My brother, who is a few years older than me, went to the same kind of school. We both wanted—no, *needed*—attention, and would do anything in the world to get it. I would just try to make people laugh, but that was enough to get me into plenty of trouble. I was *the* class clown, cracking jokes all day long at anyone's expense. All I needed was one person to giggle, and I went to town.

This private school was for students who required a lot more attention to get through their studies. I never had to go to special-ed classes; instead, my classmates and I were classified as "discipline problems," and the teachers were supposed to help us calm down and get serious about our life. They were facing an uphill battle from day one.

I was in that school for years, and I never really settled down. There were times I wasn't sure who acted worse—the students or the staff. I remember seeing some of the teachers beat up the kids and then watch the kids turn around and beat up the teachers right back. There were nonstop fights in the classrooms because even some of the little kids were banging already. What was crazy to me was that this school was located on the grounds of a huge church. In my mind, church is supposed to be a peaceful place, but at times this was more like a war zone.

The level of dysfunction was crazy. It was like being in a

giant juvenile hall, and it created more of a beast in me, because everybody at the school was messed up. Every kid who had been kicked out of public school for academic or behavioral reasons had to go to this school. I was getting good grades, but I loved attention and would get into fights with the other kids. My fighting went to a whole other level once I went to that school. I have to admit, I was bad when I was there: I fought teachers, fought other students. But I had to fight. I had to survive. I wasn't fighting everything in sight, but if you're a pit bull and you're in a corner, you've got to fight your way out.

At this private behavioral school, the carrot they dangled in front of us was called dual enrollment. If you were doing real well academically and behaving yourself, then they gave you a chance to go to public school for half a day and then back to private school for the other half. A few students made it to dual enrollment every year, but for the most part it seemed like they didn't want many kids to go to public school, and I felt pretty much brainwashed to believe that I wouldn't be able to survive in public school, so academic success was never something I aspired to. Most students never made it to public school, including me. It was hard to not be bad in that school because if you didn't step up and protect yourself, then you were looked at as a punk or like you were soft and you'd be a bigger target. In that situation I felt like there was no such thing as staying out of trouble.

Unfortunately, my home was anything but a sanctuary. After Mr. Charlie passed away, my mama met a man whom I'll refer to as Bernard. Bernard was a total character. He thought he was the coolest dude in the hood, with his chest hair peeking out of his shirt, jewelry, and general swagger. He was the type of guy the ladies gravitated toward, and I think my mama felt lucky that he chose her, despite all the negativity that seemed to follow him wherever he went. It was tough for my mom without Mr. Charlie around anymore. She was lonely, and wanted to have a man back in her life again to fill that void. Despite his many faults, Bernard fit the bill.

Bernard was handsome and charming but I just thought he was the absolute worst person on earth. I don't know how he and my moms met, but I think her confidence had already been shattered because of everything she had experienced, and so whatever the hell Bernard wanted to put her through she just dealt with. We came to find out that not only did Bernard drink but he also smoked crack. He would run off for a while and then he would come back and not be on crack for a while and then he'd go off and do it again. Bernard was incredibly abusive toward my mom and the two of them would argue for hours on end while getting drunk. To all of us kids, and to any rational person, it was the definition of a dysfunctional relationship on every possible level. The worst part about it for my siblings and me was that she always took his side in every single dispute, no matter how big or small. When Bernard came to visit he thought he was the king of the house, and everyone knew it. All of our years together as a family before Bernard entered the picture were thrown out the window. When I made my film debut as an actor in *Baby Boy*, I felt like it was everything but a movie. It was my life story being played out on film for the world to see. No, I didn't have kids like my character, Jody, but Ving Rhames's character, Melvin, was the Bernard of my house.

In a strange way, being so far removed from it now, I understand the role my mama's boyfriends and ex-husbands played in my development, and I realize that I might not have gotten out of Watts without them. They became my anti-role-models, everything I *didn't* want to become.

If I learned anything from those early years, it's that within the bad, there is always the good. For me, the good was a woman named Angie, who drove my bus to private school. Angie instantly took a liking to me, and I will remember her kindness for the rest of my life. She picked me up every single morning in a big yellow school bus, the highlight of my entire day. I would tell her about what was going on in my life. Angie had kids, but sometimes I felt like she considered me another one of her children. She even brought me to church with her family on some Sundays.

There were days when Angie would feed me and bring me new clothes to wear to school. This was usually anything extra that her son grew out of, but one day she took me to the Slauson Swap Meet to buy a few things. It wasn't much, only T-shirts and jeans, but it meant the world to me. For the first time in my life, I felt embraced. I felt loved because someone decided to spend that much time and money on me out of the blue. On a bus driver's salary, too.

She said something to me like, "Don't tell anybody that I'm buying you this stuff because I don't want the other kids to think I'm giving you special treatment. I'm not supposed to give anyone my personal phone numbers, or pick you up on the weekends, but I see something in you. You're a really smart kid and I see that you have real potential to be something in life. I'm going to help you."

Angie recognized the good in me in the midst of all the madness. She knew what was happening in my house and I think that's why her heart went out to me; she could have gotten fired for coming to pick me up. God has favor on some people's lives, and I can't explain, even right now as a grown man, why some people wanted to look out for me.

I sometimes went to church with Angie, but around the time I was twelve or thirteen I started attending Praises of Zion Baptist Church. My life was about trying to find every outlet to get away from my house, so when I heard from a neighbor that a van would pick us up to take us to the church, I grabbed the opportunity. It was at Praises of Zion that I started understanding the Word of God and lessons of the Christian gospel, appreciating it, and realizing how much it all made sense. For the first time ever the pastor's words were having an effect on me. I was in a church with at least two hundred other people but I felt like I was the only one there because it seemed like everything the pastor was saying was directed only at me. It was almost like he knew what I was thinking and was reading my mind—and he had the answers. It was the first time God was speaking directly to me through a pastor.

*　　*　　*

Pretty much everywhere you went in the hood was someone's territory, and they weren't shy about letting you know. I lived in a few different parts of Watts and there were a lot of gangs dangerously close to each other throughout the hood. With all these gangs and gangstas stacked right on top of one another, it never took long for things to set off. Some images that stick out in my memory from those days are of my mother forcing us down under the table at least a couple times a week as gunfights raged in our neighborhood and sometimes right outside our door. I once disobeyed my mama's orders by peeking out of the curtains and saw a neighbor blasting an AK-47 down the street at fleeing cars. The next morning I found a sea of bullet casings covering the street, as if World War III had taken place in front of our house.

During that time I saw a lot of drug dealers digging crack out of their asses and selling weed and dope out of their stashes to the dope fiends and weed heads. They sold pounds and pounds of weed, and some of the homeys had safes full of money from selling that shit. Cars would pull up to a well-known spot and you could drive through and get a nickel, a dime, or a dub sack worth of weed.

I never officially gangbanged, but I did a lot of crazy things that gangstas in my hood were doing. As a kid, peer pressure like that is almost impossible to ignore. I would throw up gang signs and talk the way gangstas talk. I grew up in all-Crip hoods, so every other word was "cuzz."

Wassup, cuzz?

As a kid, you just want to belong, and that's what the gangs prey on. Like a drug, they hook you when you're young, and never let you go.

When you're in the hood and you don't have family or even if you *do* have family, you can sometimes feel alone, very vulnerable, and unprotected. But when you're in a gang, you feel like everybody's got each other's backs, that you're a part of something. The streets are your family. You don't have to run around by yourself anymore, you've got somebody to talk to, somebody to laugh with. I couldn't talk to my mama and my daddy wasn't there. I would unload on my boys and we'd swap ghetto stories about our never-ending family dramas. In a gang, you've got homeys to run the streets with and get into some trouble with. Everybody protects each other.

Although most dudes in the hood are making bad choices—shooting, killing, banging, dope slinging—it's consistent that everybody loves Jesus and has a relationship with God. They may not exercise it and go to church every Sunday, but they pray and ask God for protection while they're out there doing stupid shit. I realized this, even as a youngsta. In the hood, on every Easter, Christmas, and New Year's we'd see all the thugs in their best suits, going to church to praise God. Contrary to what you see in the news, every thug loves Jesus.

I wasn't too young to join the gang—kids younger than me were already banging. There are accidental gangbangers and guys who are determined to gangbang. I would have become an accidental gangsta had an OG—that's "original gangsta"—named Dirtbike Fred not kicked me in my ass and told me to get out of there. We'd throw up gang signs and do the Crip walk and try to hang out with them, but Fred wasn't having it.

Every time he caught us trying to hang he would literally kick us in our asses. He'd tell us, *This is what we do, y'all need to get the fuck out of here, go play sports, football, basketball.* He wanted us to do anything that was different than what he and his homeys were doing.

Fred was trying to keep us out of the gangs. He didn't do it out of respect for our parents, he just did it out of respect for us. Fred had to be about forty. Now that I'm older I realize he probably knew that when you're young and trying to figure out who and what you want to be, you can be easily influenced by the glam, all the nice cars, and other stuff gangstas were buying with the drug money they were making, whether it was by hook or crook. I could have banged whether Dirtbike Fred wanted us to do it or not, and a lot of my friends ended up doing it anyway.

I never sold drugs but I was that guy hustling all across the board. If you didn't grow up in the hood, let me explain something to you: When you're broke and hungry, you've got to have hustle in order to survive. A hustle can take many forms, and it doesn't necessarily have to be a bad thing. It's just about trying to make something out of nothing any way you can. Being broke and hungry can motivate you to do *a lot* of shit.

When I was about ten, I started hustling for coins in a supermarket parking lot in Southgate, which was about five miles from our house. The supermarket wanted people to return its shopping carts because so many people would steal them, so they gave their shoppers a quarter to put the carts back. On a good night, shoppers at the local store would allow a starving kid to return their cart and get their twenty-five cents for the task. But on most nights people just looked the other way, thinking that I was some punk out to rip them off, or worse. There is nothing more humiliating in life than being a ten-year-old kid, and having strangers tell you "no" over a quarter. That's pretty much as humiliating as it gets. On the bad nights, I didn't take the bus home or eat anything at all. I walked back to Watts and went to sleep hungry.

I did anything I could to get money. Any odd job you could think of, I probably worked it. I begged at the gas station, waiting to ask people to pump their gas. I cut grass, I did landscaping. I would clean the drug man's crib and wash his car, anything so he would give me some money. I was just hungry.

We had a neighbor who always seemed to have change in his car. Every time he pulled up to his house my brother, my boy Porky, and I had a competition to see who could open the small gates of his driveway. This guy would give us whatever change he had—seven or ten or thirty-five cents—and we'd wait for the ice cream truck to spend the money he gave us. With whatever change I had left after I bought food for myself, it all went to candy—I used to love to eat sunflower seeds, Chick-O-Stix, Lemonheads, Boston Baked Beans, Strawberry Shortcake ice cream bars, Pink Panther ice cream, ice cream sandwiches, and Red Vines.

When I was about ten I worked on an ice cream truck for a family-owned business. I rode around with an African woman, helping her sell ice cream; her husband drove one truck and had one or two of their kids with him and she had another couple of kids and me. I figured out what I thought was a creative way to steal money and the balloons they gave out to kids: I just put it all in my pockets. I thought I was being all slick, but one day she saw me through the rearview mirror. She pulled over the truck and in her thick accent she said, "Ty-dese, you steal my money! What is in your pocket?" She made me pull out the insides of my pockets and all the money fell out along with the balloons. There were so many—red, white, blue, yellow, green, and pink balloons—all over the ground so I could barely see my feet. She fired me on the spot and cursed me out while she drove me home. Before I got off the truck, I turned around and asked, "Do you mind if I have those balloons?" She yelled, "No! Get off my truck!" And I walked up to my house empty-handed.

In my early teens I did a whole lot of stealing. I stole clothing off clothing lines so I could have a fresh T-shirt, underwear, jeans, and socks. Every other night we would go five, six or seven yards over and just hop over the fence. My homeys and I jacked some Mexicans for their bikes. We used to go to Southgate, and we'd see a Mexican on his bike and just beat him up and ride back on his bike. We got caught a few times and ended up on probation.

My boys and I were just rough—with our bikes or whatever toys we had. We had one bike and would ride around on it for months. We would mess up a bike so bad that both tires would go flat and since we couldn't afford new ones, we'd just ride around on the rims and our hands would go numb from holding on to the vibrating handlebars. We would push each other in shopping carts from the shopping center, wilding out and having fun. We did anything to have fun in the midst of a crazy situation. That's why they say, *It's all good in the hood, baby.*

In 1992, the news of the acquittal of the four officers who

had beaten Rodney King enraged everybody, and they sparked the LA Riots. I was only thirteen, but I had seen on television that everyone in the hood was out looting so I went out with the rest of them, stealing shit out of swap meets and stores—I was popping. For two days I went around with my boys in a big hatchback truck. Buildings everywhere were on fire, and it was so hot that we could feel the heat off the buildings as we drove by. I was afraid the whole time we were doing it—the scene was nuts. My heart was beating hard but I stayed out because it was a free-for-all. At one point, we went into a grocery store and because of the fires, the sprinkler system had left about three feet of water on the floor, so we had to step through the large puddles as we collected some food. The riots and looting weren't just about Rodney King. They were about ongoing racism that had been brewing for years and finally reached a tipping point and exploded on the streets of South Central LA. Mexicans were fighting with the blacks, and any white or Asian person was a target. We went to places the Asians owned, like the swap meets. They were spray-painting "Black-owned business" across their storefronts because they thought it would stop people from looting and burning down their stores, but they got looted anyway because anyone who lived in the hood knew exactly which stores had black owners. The news started reporting that the National Guard was shooting at people with dummy bullets and my moms didn't let us go out after that.

Years later when I was in high school, O. J. Simpson was acquitted for his wife's death. That trial was on television all day every day, and as soon as they announced the verdict my boys and a few of my homegirls went down the streets screaming because a black guy had been let off. We had all thought that if he didn't get acquitted it would all go down again in the hood, that there would be more riots. Everybody knew that the verdict was coming in so police were everywhere wearing their riot gear. They were prepared to deal with everything just in case people started looting. But we all know nothing happened because white folks weren't going to start burning down Beverly Hills. At the end of the day, most of the blacks and Latinos who were rooting for O.J. to get off weren't really paying attention to the facts or what was being reported. We just all felt that this was another black man who was wrongly accused, because we were always being accused. So we wanted to celebrate his acquittal.

Living in the hood, I still had a lot of fun. We had to make the best of a bad situation and environment and that's what we did. We had the time of our lives—willying our bikes in the streets, football and basketball games, playing baseball in the park, going to the mall, to the swap meet, running track, having water balloon fights, riding on the backs of ice cream trucks, swimming at Will Rogers Park and in Jacuzzis and swimming pools around the hood, hitting talent shows at the park, flirting, having fun with girls. One of my favorite childhood games with my boys and girls was called Hide Go Get It; when you found the girl you'd get to dry hump on her—fun times! We would take slabs of drywall from a new house they were building and with the white chalk inside it, draw lines in the middle of the street like a real football field and play for hours. We'd also draw out basketball courts in the middle of the street, and use bicycle tires as basketball hoops.

You name it, we did it, and we had a great time and I don't want anyone to think any different. And my family still laughed. My siblings, mama, and I cracked jokes and got silly— nobody made us laugh the way we made each other laugh. I was the king of all kings when it came to anything funny in my house. Everything was messed up but every chance we got we'd just try and make the best of a bad reality. We watched *Def Comedy Jam* when it first came out and completely submerged ourselves in comedy shows as an outlet so that everything wasn't as heavy all day, every day. I still have a lot of love for the hood. I don't want to cast a cloud as if there is nothing positive about it because there is. And visually, Watts is a beautiful place, compared to some of the other hoods in the country and places I've been since I've been able to see the world.

But in the midst of all the fun my friends and I had, there were a whole lot of killings, a whole lot of drugs and gang-banging happening. My household was like a pot of stew that had every combination of emotion in it. Being hungry, seeing my mama drink and get beat, I felt helpless most of the time because I couldn't do anything. It was heaven and hell in a pot, and it just kept on stirring. Any day you could go from having the time of your life, to coming out of your front door and seeing one of your homeboys under a sheet right there on your block—and you could have just been laughing and having fun with him the day before. It's crazy to think that when Daniel and I played our games and used a little piece of something we found on the floor as a gun and said *pow pow pow*, right down the street my big homeys were using real guns, and the *pow* that we heard meant a bullet was shot, and that bullet was taking a life. Moments like that reminded me that I needed to get out of there. That was it. It was eat or be eaten. I would have been sucked into the matrix if I hadn't decided there *had* to be something else out there better for me.

When I was a kid I sang pretty much everywhere I went, around the house, in the shower. I didn't think for a second that I was any good because nobody in my family ever complimented me on my voice or told me I could sing. In fact, all I ever heard was, "Tyrese, why don't you shut up?" Or, "Tyrese, why are you making so much noise?" So when my neighbor heard me singing one day when I was thirteen, the last thing I expected her to do was ask me to sing for her, which is what she did. She went nuts. She responded in a way I had never heard before. She said, "Tyrese, you can sing! You can sing real good!" Not long after that, she had a big party at her house and invited a bunch of her girlfriends and cousins over, and I sang for them in her front yard. They reacted the same way my neighbor did, but I was still trying to figure out if they were saying such nice things just because I was a kid, or because they really meant it.

I didn't think I had any talent that could specifically help get me out of Watts until my neighbor heard me sing. She kind of planted the idea in me that music was something I needed to look into. As soon as she and her friends told me I could sing, I was going to try and go all the way—period. If singing could get me out of Watts, I was going to put all my time and energy into music and singing. The pain of being broke, hungry, stuck without a ride or any transportation, the feeling of being vulnerable and being in an unpredictable environment became my motivation.

It didn't take long for me to be singing for my neighbor and her friends on a regular basis. To change things up I decided to do it for some different people, because I had already won those women over, and I needed to see if my singing impressed people who didn't just live on my street. So I entered the Head Start Talent Show at Will Rogers Park with four of my boys; I sang lead vocals on a New Edition song with them doing harmony. I sang my heart out and we finished in first place.

If you asked me back then if I was going to go far with music, I'd have told you I had no idea. But I would have also said to you that *anything* would be better than the shit I was living in. I had *decided* I wanted better for my life, my surroundings, and everything else. I was always thinking, *I need to get out of here*. I'm *broke*, I'm *hungry*, there is nothing that I'm wearing on my back that was purchased, it was either given to me or a hand-me-down or some stuff Bernard brought home, or something stolen off a clothing line. I don't really know if that was an epiphany or just literally *knowing* there had to be something else out here that was better, and so whatever the hell I had to do to get money and hustle to get out of there, I did. I would have tap-danced in front of the Cheesecake Factory.

After I won first place I was singing and practicing every chance I got. I would sing in the bathroom into a little tape recorder, because the bathroom had better reverb and echo.

I was trying to figure out my voice and if I was hitting good notes or bad notes.

Don Lee would also tell me to come to the gym at Will Rogers Park and I would sing for hours along with a karaoke machine. He would play song instrumentals and record me on the other side, so technically that was my first time ever getting recorded. I was there every other day, singing and learning my first bit of choreography. Don had a little Motown going on up at the park where he had discovered and was working on developing a few other groups that were pretty big in our community at the time, like Y.N.V., J'Son, and the Fellaz. They would perform at talent showcases and the girls would just go nuts.

One night I was watching *Midnight Love* on BET, and I decided to write down all the record labels that the artists who appeared were signed to. I wrote down every record label, every music video, and then I wrote down all the different record labels I could think of off the top of my head. After that, I started calling every one and told them the same story. I said, "Hi. My name is Tyrese, I'm fourteen, I'm from Watts, and I want to be a singer, I want to get a record deal." They all told me the same thing—that they don't take solicitations over the phone and that I should send them my demo. I borrowed tapes from my neighbors or popped the bottoms off of prerecorded tapes so I could dub over them. I got ahold of some stamps, and started sending out my demo.

When I called Priority Records, Gayle Atkins picked up the phone. The crazy thing is, it wasn't even her phone. I had called into the general line. Gayle's friend—who normally answered the phone—had asked Gayle to answer her line because she was expecting a really important call. If Gayle hadn't answered the phone I probably would have heard the same speech I had gotten from every other label—that they don't take solicitations. It was by design that she was at the front desk sitting in for her friend.

Gayle didn't work in A&R, she worked in promotions, and when she answered, I hit her with the same thing: "Hi. My name is Tyrese, I'm from Watts, I'm young, I wanna sing, I wanna be a great singer when I grow up one day, and I want a record deal. I know that Priority Records has got artists and I'm just wondering if…" And Gayle said, "Oh yeah? You're a singer? Well, sing something." I was shocked that she asked me to sing—that she wasn't turning me away. That was my fourteenth phone call. I had been on the phone all day. So I ran to the bathroom and sang for her over the phone, and she said, "Wow, you sound good. You've got a really nice voice." We ended up communicating. I sent her letters, demo tapes of me singing in the bathroom and lyric sheets I had written out, and I think her heart went out to me.

About two months later she ended up coming to the hood to meet me. Now, when I first talked to Gayle I thought she was a white girl. She is a really attractive woman, a black girl who grew up in the Valley, so she speaks extremely articulately. She was saying, "Oh my God, you're so cute. You're really talented. I was just wondering what I could do for you." Originally she was not interested in managing me on any level. She had just figured that since she knew a few people in the music business, maybe she could help me out.

Gayle would come to get me almost every weekend. A few times she took me up to the home of Paul Stewart, one of the head guys at Priority Records, who lived in a huge house in the Hollywood Hills, right next to the piano player George Duke. I swam in his pool, messed with his turntables, ran through his house. I knew it was a big deal for me to be in this huge place doing all this stuff, because I'm from the bottom-of-the-barrel Watts. I had never been to anybody's house that was that big, I had never met or even seen people who owned or lived in houses that big. Looking at this guy—he's rich, living in the Hollywood Hills—I realized there was so much more to reach for. Unfortunately, when you're in the hood you tend to want to become the things you see—the same is true for anyone, no matter where you are—but when I was exposed to this new world, I started realizing there was more out there. Gayle created a huge shift in my life. She became an important person in my formative years as a musician and as a man. Gayle introduced me to amazing people, like Greg Parks, who managed me for years and years. Like my bus driver Angie, Gayle was a supportive and caring mother figure in my life.

But I wasn't with Gayle all the time. I still lived in Watts and went to the private school. By this point I had moved on to ninth grade in the high school section.

The principal was a kindhearted white man who I could tell cared about each and every student at the school. His door was always open, and he gave me his home and cell phone numbers in case I ever needed help. He was a good role model for me in the midst of all the chaos of school and my home. I could tell he understood the complexities of life that his students faced. He was honest and went the extra mile for me. Thinking back on it, he was the first white person who had ever cared for me, and I count him as the person who broke down my own personal color barrier. Up to that point, the only white people I had ever seen in my neighborhood were police officers, firefighters, doctors, or those guys who check electric meters. Of course, none of those people actually lived where we did. It was just the Latinos and us, for the most part, so I never experienced anyone outside of my race caring about me. But after I met him, I never saw color. I just saw people.

I remember being a little scared to go to high school, but I continued to use my power to win over people who should have been my enemies. Since I wasn't banging, I wasn't trying to be hard and gangsta like everybody else, and I figured if I was funny and got everybody laughing, nobody would try and beat me up or mess with me. If you're not a threat, nobody will try to take anything from you—you're harmless. And, for the most part, it worked. My humor became my strength against a lot of these realities, including the feeling that I was never going to get out of that damn school.

I did try to maintain a positive attitude but I still got into fights. They were a way of channeling my anger at being extremely scared and freaked out about the things I couldn't control in my life. I had no control over what was going to happen at my house, or my day or night, but I had to go home because that's where I lived. It was completely in their hands and that drove me nuts.

Some time in the early part of ninth grade I got into a big fight with one of the teachers who beat me up really bad. I came home with bruises on my face and knowing nothing would happen or change, I called the police on the school. By doing that I became a threat, because I could potentially expose what some of the teachers were doing to the kids, and they kicked me out. At the end of the day, I had such a history of fights like most of the kids there, so even if I had tried to go full-on and get a lawyer, nothing would have happened, because back then the school was for kids with behavioral problems.

I had been up for dual enrollment in high school as well, but I never made it because I was too bad and dysfunctional. So they never allowed me to go to public school for even half a day. Once I got kicked out of the behavioral school and knew I'd be going to Locke High School I didn't think I'd be able to stay out of trouble. When I first arrived at Locke's big campus, I thought I was so bad that I couldn't believe they even allowed me to check in. I remember standing in the office with my moms, praying they would let me in, and being totally shocked when they let me register. I remember thinking, *What do you mean, I can go straight back into public school?!* I had been kicked out of public elementary school when I was young, went to a private school and got kicked out of there, too. My record was even worse than before I had left public school in the first place. I felt like I had two strikes against me, so it seemed crazy to me that they let me right back into public school. And because many of my former teachers had made me believe I wouldn't make it in public school, I was worried I wouldn't be able to survive at Locke.

But I was fine. It was like I was out of jail and able to be among society, and everything that some of the teachers at private school had told me I was or wasn't ended up being the total opposite. There were kids at Locke High School who were bad as hell but that wasn't me. I was on my p's and q's. For the first five or six months I was making good grades, going through the typical awkward stage of getting acquainted. Once I got comfortable, I started being my usual self—cracking jokes, acting all silly and funny, making friends, being the center of attention. I had always thought that the world was my stage and all of a sudden, my stage had gotten bigger. Sure, I still got into some trouble for skipping class, running in the hallways, putting up graffiti and getting into minor fights, but mentally I was in a better place.

I was able to interact and learn and readjust myself to being around regular folks and doing regular things. And I was finally able to make use of my talent. The first class I signed up for was music with Reggie Andrews. I went straight into his classroom on the first day of school and got into a friendly competition with my boy Timothy Jackson and we ended up just singing all the time. I could finally channel my energy in a good way and make use of my love for singing and songwriting. I was learning music and how to play the piano and drums.

Every morning I was desperate to get to school. I loved going because it was where I could eat, and for six or seven hours I was able to forget the reality of what went on in my house. I still hustled quarters and did odd jobs, because I needed change to take the bus to school in the morning. On the mornings I didn't have change for the bus, I missed Angie picking me up even more.

In LA, when I was a kid, there were two types of buses. There was the RTD, which took you farther, but cost $1.10 each way. Then there was the DASH bus, which covered less ground, but was only twenty-five cents. On top of that, the RTD was more sophisticated. It had an automated change counter, which showed the bus driver how much money you put in. The DASH only had a metal tray that you tossed change into, and sometimes just the sound of coins clinking in the tray was enough to satisfy the driver and get you on board.

The problem was, on many days I didn't have a single coin to clink in the tray, and on those mornings I would get a crick in my neck from looking for change on the ground as I walked to the bus stop. Fortunately, there was one driver who always let me on the bus whether I had the fare or not. But she was only one of many drivers on my route, and on the mornings I didn't have any money I would have to get to the bus stop really early to catch her, because the other drivers would slam the door in my face when I told them I didn't have any money. It was either that, wait more than an hour for her to circle the route and get to school late, or walk the three miles to school. Considering where I lived, I would have had to walk through at least ten to twelve different gang territories to get to school and that wasn't always a comfortable thought.

I would wake up early and walk to the bus stop at 103rd and Success Avenue. Directly behind the stop was a giant tree, with branches that hung over the sidewalk and above the street. I would stand at the stop, squinting through the sun to see the early-morning bus coming down the street toward me, trying desperately to make out if my lucky driver was behind the wheel. The sun was usually so bright that I couldn't make out who the driver was until a few seconds before the bus pulled up to the curb. If I was out of luck, the doors would swing open, and I would just stand there, head hanging in shame as the driver asked me if I was getting on. When I'd tell him that I didn't have any money, he would close the doors without saying anything, leaving me on the curb. As it pulled away, the bus would scrape the branches of the tree behind me, so its leaves would fall to the ground. Then the bus engine would blow out a plume of exhaust, making the dust and the dirt and the leaves shoot up from the ground in the direction of anyone sitting at the bus stop. I would sit back on the bench and wait to reenact that same scene until the second angelic bus driver in my life showed up.

I would think, *Getting to school should not be harder than school itself. No wonder there are so many dropouts. When it's this difficult, how do they expect kids to show up?* I wanted to go to school and get an education, I didn't want to be a dropout. All I wanted was to escape the pain that was waiting for me back home, but the public transportation system was making that impossible. I had to miss school a few days because I couldn't get a ride or hadn't slept the night before. No child should miss school because they can't get there. And there I was, standing at the bus stop, not banging, not dope-slinging, not shooting, and not killing, I was just trying to get to school and I didn't have a quarter. *Twenty— five pennies.* My thinking was, *I'm a good person. I'm not a killer. I'm not crazy, I never went to jail. I'm just in the hood, so why am I struggling this hard?* You would think that because you're a good person in the midst of all this madness that things would be better for you. And then you see the dope dealers driving up the street in their nice cars with a loud sound system and girls in the front seat. You know they have on the latest Nikes and the fresh white T-shirts and the jewelry, and the cell phones. Waiting for the bus, trying to get to school, you can't help but think, *Man, if I start doing some of the shit that they're doing then maybe I'll get some of the money they're getting. Because trying to do it the right way is just not paying off fast enough.* That's why most of the cats in the hood jump off into the dope game. But I didn't want to gangbang—there were too many people dying and I didn't want to die. And I loved going to school.

I found out after I arrived at Locke that there was a great musical tradition there. Reggie Andrews, my teacher, inspired me—he fed me when I was hungry and he was a father figure because he gave me advice on some of the stuff I was dealing with at home. He was my sounding board. Reggie was also a well-known producer. He had written "Let It Whip," a hit song made famous by the Dazz Band, and many famous musicians had graduated from my school: Rickey Minor, a bass player and one of the most famous music directors in the country; Patrice Rushen, who sang "Forget Me Nots"; Gerald Albright, the saxophone player; and the whole trumpet section from Earth, Wind & Fire. All these legends went to my high school. The music department at Locke was a testament to Reggie Andrews being a great teacher.

Because of that tradition, one day some folks called my high school and said they were looking for a male black kid for a national Coke commercial. Since I was sixteen, about the age of the kid they wanted, Reggie told me about it. I didn't have money to take the bus across town to get to the audition, so Reggie said he would take me himself. I just had to wait for him to finish teaching and lock up the music department. When we finally got to the audition, we were almost three hours late. The woman running the auditions was still there, but she was all packed and ready to go; she was just waiting for her ride, who was stuck in traffic. When I asked her if I could still sing for her, she was very cold and firm and said, "You're late, I'm sorry." I started apologizing to her, explaining that I didn't have a ride, and Reggie backed me up, telling her that we were late because I had to wait for him, that I was from the hood and didn't have money for transportation, otherwise I would have been there earlier. She sympathized with me and with an attitude, sighed and said, "All right, just warm up."

I started singing and she looked at me with her eyes lit up. She started unpacking her equipment; she pulled out a camera, gave me a pair of headphones, and put a backpack on me. I sang Montell Jordan's "This Is How We Do It" so I could dance while I was singing, and then I did two or three of my favorite songs. She asked me to improvise some Coca-Cola jingles, and as I did I was smiling and laughing—I was doing pretty much whatever she asked me to do, and then some.

She told me I was amazing, but I didn't know what that meant because it was my first audition. I had extremely low expectations because up until that point in my life, the major things I had tried to do had not happened on any level. I wanted a record deal, but people kept turning me down or weren't returning my phone calls. I was excited that I had been able to audition, but I was still negative about it. I didn't really believe that the woman was really going to show the tapes of my audition to her associates. I knew it would be a national commercial, I knew they had auditioned kids in all the major cities, and that Los Angeles was the last location and I was literally the last person to show up. I didn't believe it would happen for me. As Reggie drove me home, he kept telling me that I had done a great job, but I was thinking there was no way they would choose me for it. Now that I've gotten older I am able to see that it was all a part of God's plan. Four days later I found out I got the gig. The commercial was a hit and got such a great response that they took it international.

Years later, I realized how crazy it was that in the commercial that sparked my career I was singing on a bus—a bus just like the one I had to take every day, a bus I usually couldn't afford, that represented many of my childhood struggles. Because of that commercial, I never had to take the bus again.

I don't usually talk about my childhood because it's mostly bad memories. I don't want to sit up and be reminded of all this stuff that I love to forget, because you can't get points today for yesterday's game—whatever happened yesterday is over. Today is a new day. So many people are submerged in what *was*, they don't even focus on *now*. They don't focus on the future. Every time they look back they cry and have all this pain about their past.

I know that the dysfunction I was exposed to as a child made me who I am. I like to say that every lesson is a blessing. I don't think I would be this passionate about life, and I don't think my work ethic would be the way it is, if my childhood had been nice and peaceful. It wouldn't have created the motivation in me to want something different for my life.

I use my messed-up childhood to keep me motivated and to keep my life and career moving forward because I know that hell is out there. I don't sit around and dwell on my past, and that way I'm able to get out of my own way, because to hold on to the past limits your future. I'm using my past as a part of my determination to never experience my past again.

Chapter 2

How Much Do You Love Yourself?

This book is called *How to Get Out of Your Own Way*, and I want you to really think about that for a minute. What does that mean to you? Have you ever let opportunities pass you by because you didn't think you were good enough or worthy enough to take them? Have you ever allowed others to prevent you from improving your life? Have you ever stopped *yourself* from sorting out a problem? Most of the things that I'll be speaking about are adjustments I've made in my own life, things that I've been able to see and recognize and stop doing. You *can* get in front of your problems and get in control of your life and make it better. Hopefully something you read here will give you permission to want better for yourself, because getting to whatever that better spot is should be the ultimate mission of your life.

The one mission I had when I was young was to get out of the hood. I decided that I wanted better for myself and that I didn't want to be like anybody around me. I wanted my life to be the complete opposite of everything and most of the people I grew up around. I decided to fall in love with who I am. I didn't know it, but even back then I was trying to get out of my own way.

There wasn't a specific time or date or *monumental moment* when I knew I had to get out of there. For me, the process of getting out of my own way happens moment by moment. When each moment presents itself, I can decide to do something wrong—if I was already made aware that it was wrong—or I can do it right. When you know there are better circumstances you can be in, or that there's a better way to do something, and you decide right then and there you want better for yourself and do it right, that's when you're technically getting out of your own way.

But it's not as easy as that because your life decisions boil down to how you see yourself and how much you love and value yourself. Your actions reflect what you want for yourself and what you feel you *deserve*. I grew up with a few people who didn't think they deserved anything and that's the way some of them are still living. Everything I was doing when I was living in the hood shows how much I loved myself: I loved myself too much to keep living like that. I loved myself too much to not try and hustle for quarters for food or call every record label to get a record deal. You can think about this in all areas of your life: I love myself too much to date someone like you. I love myself too much to keep sitting on my ass instead of searching for a new job. I love myself too much to have unprotected sex, or to keep friends in my life who bring me down.

We need to find out how much we love ourselves in order to get out of our own way. Part of that is accepting our flaws. It sounds contradictory, but you have to see the truth of who you are in order to get in front of the problem. How can you ever understand your actions and try to change until you take a good look at the choices you've made? How can you open up a line of communication with yourself or others about your actions and try to change? You have to figure out why you keep staying on the wrong path and making the wrong decisions.

One of my favorite quotes that really shook me up when I

heard it was, "You'll never know who you *are* till you discover who you're *not*." It made me feel more comfortable with accepting my flaws. How can I make any changes in my life if I'm not in tune with the way I feel about myself?

You have to come clean with yourself. You've got to be an open book. You've got to allow people to see into you and you've got to put all your flaws on the table, especially the things you don't understand. You've got to be vulnerable and be willing to accept some of the worst things you could ever hear about yourself, especially if you've been messing up. This is something I went through myself and it was *tough*—like my whole world crashed in—but I'm a better man for it. When you start to look back and accept your bad choices along with the good, learn from them, and start to love yourself enough, you'll begin to get in front of it and out of your own way.

If you have a problem with your life, you can elevate yourself or keep standing still, but you will have to decide if you're going to change. I've said this to many people: *Life is a menu. Whoever and whatever you order for your life is what's going to be delivered to the table.* If you want something new or better for your life, you have to order it. *You* are responsible for where you are in your life. You have more influence and can make more of a difference than you can ever imagine, but it has to start with you. When people are going through hell, they say, *God will get me through this*, but God also gave us free will. He puts us in a scenario and we must decide on our own what we're going to do. You can get on your knees and pray but prayers shouldn't be your only course of action. Most Christians can go to church and be saved but because God gave us free will, it's *your* choice to save yourself from drama, craziness, dysfunctional surroundings, and bad personal and business relationships. You have to stop getting into the wrong situations and start making better decisions.

Your life is the life *you* choose to live. If your life is miserable, is it because you're too lazy to change? You have to create the reality *you* want. If you're complaining every day that you have a problem with your life, you must do something about it. Too many people choose not to. But you have to stop complaining if you're not going to try and change. If you *really* had a problem, you would do something about it, right?

When we have problems in our life we have two choices. We could sit around and pity ourselves, cry about our misfortunes, and accept our fates. That is not me, and that has never been what I am about. I got to where I am now by never being satisfied with my current situation, and I always want more out of life. So I choose the second option—to change. I love myself too much to accept anything less than the absolute best out of life, and I want you to feel the same way.

It's easy to pity ourselves. It's easier to think that all the unfortunate things that happen to us and all the bad situations we find ourselves in are completely out of our hands, that we are simply victims of a cruel fate. But these are excuses we tell ourselves because we are afraid to accept that we can control our lives. Feeling sorry for yourself is a one-way ticket to nowhere.

You've been sitting on the pity potty long enough, so flush the toilet and try to let it go. Cry for a night, but when the sun comes up, know that you've flushed the pity potty and keep on moving. If you keep thinking of yourself as the victim, you don't understand the power you have.

If you want to stay in a hole, then that's where you *want* to be. If you want better for yourself but are not willing to try and change your circumstances, you must question how much you love yourself. You must ask yourself why you're so comfortable staying where you are. Why do you feel you don't deserve to turn your life around? Why do you not want the very best for yourself? Life is about transitioning from who we are right now into someone greater, someone better. I want you to reach for everything you can reach for. *Be* better. *Want* better. When you figure out what you want for yourself and put that energy into the universe, it will come back to you eventually, like when you throw a pebble into water, the water vibrates and ripples outward. So jump into the water. Sometimes it's frozen and it looks impossible, but take the leap of faith, jump in, and watch the water move around you.

Change is hard and it can be scary, but the effort is worth it. Every person that improved his or her life made the choice and did something about it. If you're afraid, for whatever reason, remember that *a saint is a sinner that got up.* One of my mentors, John Bryant, told me that once and I've never forgotten it. It reminds me that we all go through trials—even saints—and that we all have the opportunity to become better. A person may be considered a sinner because of their bad choices and the negative way they decided to lead their life. At some point even your pastor was sinning, but he *got up* and rededicated his life to Christ and decided to live and walk with God. In the same way, before you realized you could change, you were "sinning." You were making bad choices, you were doing bad things to yourself or other people, and you weren't moving your life forward, but once you *get up* and make the decision to change, you will be following in the path of the saints. When I heard that quote it just made me feel good, because a lot of us hold on to what *was* and can't let go of the bad choices we made. We often don't remember that even saints made mistakes. As long as you're not *continuing* to do wrong, whatever you did is now in the past. If you start to change and make better choices for yourself, you can seal the coffin on your past actions. You're living righteously *now* and trying your best to live better *now*, because you *got up*. You're not doing what you used to do, because you learned from it.

You should do everything possible to try and turn your life around. I am still not comfortable where I am, and I know I've come a long way. I am asking you to *get up* and love yourself more.

Your Body Is a Slave of the Mind

One of the first things you have to know as you start to make changes in your life and get out of your own way is that it all starts in your mind. This sounds obvious but there's more to it than just thinking *I need to change*. You need to change your actions. Everything you think, do, and say is a result of how much you love yourself, and how much you love yourself depends on your *mind-set*. If your mind-set changes, everything in your life can change, too. The day you start thinking differently your life will become different.

This is because your body is a slave of the mind. Your body is going to do what your mind tells it to do. For example, when you drive a car, your mind says, *Make a left*, and your body responds by turning the steering wheel to the left. Whatever you do, you thought of it first, and like a puppet, your body does exactly what your mind tells it to do. You must first think it or feel it before you speak it. Whatever you do, however you act, whatever you wear, however you carry yourself, whom you choose to be in a relationship with, and whether you decide to change your life are all results of your thoughts and mind-set.

The idea that your body is a slave of the mind is similar to something James Allen wrote in *As a Man Thinketh*, one of the books that has influenced me the most in my life. It says, "A man is literally what he thinks, his character being the complete sum of all of his thoughts. As the plant springs from, and could not be without, the seed, so every act of man springs from the hidden seeds of thought and could not have appeared without them.... Act is the blossom of thought, and joy and suffering are its fruits." When I first read that, it impacted me in a major way. At the time, I was out of shape and knew that what I was eating wasn't good for me or my career. I had decided that I hated working out and loved food more than maintaining my body, which played a crucial part in giving me opportunities to be able to eat. My body had created all the situations where people were looking my way; Hollywood executives were calling with movie roles, I was getting offers for endorsement deals and modeling contracts, all these people wanted me to take my shirt off but I was so out of shape that I'd turn them down. And when I was on stage, I knew the girls wanted me to take off my shirt, but I was out of shape so I would just tease them and never take it off all the way. After reading *As a Man Thinketh* I realized that everything in my mind became my actions and that a person is literally what he or she thinks. I had to change how I was thinking.

If your mind-set is too negative then it will affect how willing you'll be to better yourself or your circumstances. It can create a cycle of negativity because when we're down on ourselves, we're not very motivated to improve our lives.

Do You Have a Negative Mind and Spirit?

If you are blocking yourself from making changes in your life, you are standing in your own way, and this may be because you have a negative spirit. The negative spirit comes from a negative mind-set. It's a voice that always blocks your own blessings because you can't see the positive in anything. When you're that negative, you attract dysfunctional people and stay in a *cycle* of negativity. Your opportunities for change are right there, so I want you to get rid of this negative voice.

You may be afraid of stepping out there and doing something you've never done, but take me as an example. I started my career with a thirty-second Coke commercial. I was sixteen years old and didn't have a penny to my name, but I stretched my career after that because I took a leap of faith, I stepped away from the negative spirit around me, and tried some new things. It doesn't matter what your obstacles are, if you have three or four kids or put on a little weight. You just have to take one little step to start and make it happen. All those obstacles in your path of fulfillment are only obstacles because you're telling yourself they are. If you say you can't make it, you won't. If you say you can make it, you will. You are absolutely right about both.

I wanted better and believed I could do better because it was in my spirit. I decided I loved myself enough to try. Even if you're broke financially doesn't mean your *spirit* has to be broken. You could be financially broke but rich in spirit. I learned this from my mentor John Bryant. He once said to me that there's a difference between being broke and being poor: Being poor is an economic condition that doesn't have to be permanent, but being broke is a disabling state of mind and spirit that affects all aspects of your life. If you're poor, that's only financial, but you *don't* have to be poor in your mind. There are people in prison, in cages, whose spirits are strong. So you have to make a choice: Are you going to be miserable, or are you going to be happy?

Everything that you do and everything that you channel your energy into all comes back to you because it's all linked to your mind-set and what you're thinking. Even something as simple as watching TV can affect your day. I don't watch a lot of television and I don't like watching the news, because they usually report the most negative stories all day, every day. I know it's the responsibility of a news channel to inform us about what's going on in the world, but I wish there was some way there could be more of a balance. Unfortunately, most people aren't interested in those positive stories as much as they are into the negative ones.

You should know whether you're watching the news out of curiosity to find out what's going on or watching the news because you're trying to feed the negativity in you. You may feel so negative that you're drawn to everything and everyone that's negative, including negative tabloid magazines or gossip websites and blogs. Some people go to these sites because they want to submerge themselves in negative thoughts. I would even suggest they become addicted to other people's business. If you're going to these different websites and actually sign up to write negative things about other people—whether you know them or not—what does that say about your mind-set? It's one thing to visit the sites—we all do, because we live in a media-saturated culture—but it's another thing if you go through the process and sign up for an account. By doing that, you've committed to negativity on a whole other level: Not only have you created a user name, but now you're frequently going to the site, writing your comments, and feeding the nature of the beast. You might not have a lot going on in your life and career, but by doing that you're inviting that dark energy into your life. And that very dark energy will follow you like your own shadow.

Some of the people I know who live in the hood have great jobs and money but they stay in that environment and I always wondered why until one of my teachers at Locke told me that a lot of people in the hood are institutionalized. I asked him what that meant and he explained that they may have enough money to leave but they are more comfortable staying. As gang-infested, wild, crazy, and unpredictable as it gets, a lot of people are more comfortable living there than in a safer area. In most cases, people look for great jobs to make money and get out, but there are some people who want to stay. They don't want to move out to the suburbs, away from the drama and bullshit. And even if they leave, it doesn't mean that leaving is going to make them happy. Some people may hit the lottery and wonder why they even left. Some people go more crazy from peace and serenity than from drama and bullshit; it's like they're in a prison. When my teacher told this to me, it made me think of one of the characters from the movie *The Shawshank Redemption* who was finally released from prison after fifty years. He could not survive living as a free man and ultimately took his own life. You would think that he would be jumping for joy to leave prison but it was scary for him because everything about what he had known for so many years behind bars had become a part of who he was. He was institutionalized, and felt like a fish out of water. In the same way, for many people, living in the hood is a comfort zone; it would be unfamiliar to leave. That was not the case for me. As soon as I made money, I was out.

It's all part of a cycle. The brain is like a machine, and it will adapt to whatever life you lead. Your mind will get used to negativity and think of it as normal. You will continue to block your blessings because you won't love yourself enough to change. When you are overly negative, you sabotage yourself from getting to your better place.

Self-Sabotage

The negative spirit is dangerous because it can turn you into your own worst enemy. When we sabotage ourselves, we prevent any sort of progress in our lives. As soon as you want to do something, a negative thought prevents you from doing it—it talks you out of it. As soon as something good starts happening in your life, you figure out a way—consciously or unconsciously—to mess it up. The negative spirit takes something beautiful and positive and turns it into a negative.

Once you're made aware of the right way to go about it, the right thing to say or do, and you do the complete *opposite* of that, you're purposely deciding to be in your own way because you're no longer ignorant about the situation. And you should prepare yourself for the repercussions.

A few years ago I was not aware that I was sabotaging my career. I was eating too much and had gained a lot of weight. In the movie business, your physique is part of the package and I was sabotaging myself because I knew I should not be eating the things I was eating. As I explained earlier, most of who we are as adults is somehow directly connected to our childhood, and I realized my self-sabotage went back to the fact that when I was younger, I was never able to eat, and when I did, it didn't mean I was eating what I really wanted; it just meant that was the meal provided for me, so that was what I *had* to eat. I had gone most of my life not eating what I wanted, when I wanted, and where I wanted, so once I started making money the *last* thing I wanted was someone telling me I couldn't eat what I felt like eating—because everyone makes money to do the things they really want to do. I didn't want to worry about a diet and eating healthy. A lot of people don't associate food with addiction, but in a way I was addicted to it. Food was my drug. In the same way, someone who is putting heroin in their arm knows the heroin is not good for them but they're addicted to it and they get to the point where they don't care how they look or what it's doing to their life or career.

I was in my own way because I knew I wasn't supposed to eat like that and make myself get that big. I was still eating that way *while* I was aware of the challenges and troubles I was creating for my career by being out of shape. I was sabotaging myself when I didn't stop myself from eating what I felt like eating. I valued myself but I was still struggling with that balance, and I still do. It's an everyday beast but I am now *aware* of it so I can get in front of it. The question becomes this: How can someone be rebellious against him- or herself? How can you purposely block your own blessings? I don't believe anyone sits down and consciously decides to fuck up their career or life.

People who suffer from self-sabotage and self-defeat may be suffering from a negative spirit. That is why I want you to try and *reprogram* your mind with more positive energy.

Reprogram Your Mind and Spirit

How you feel about yourself starts at home. There is power in the tongue, and your mind-set will be affected by what other people will say to you and about you. People speak two different languages. It's one thing for someone to get on you about your bad habits in a constructive way, and it's another thing to just be negative and condescending. How are the people in your life affecting you?

If your partner, your lover, parent, sibling, or teacher puts you down constantly and says you're worthless, then at some point, if you don't know any different, you are going to believe it, because you have put your faith and trust in that person. Your own thinking may be, *If they claim to care about me, then why would they say something that wasn't true?* If you don't hear how amazing you are every day at home, then when anyone tries to pay you a compliment you won't believe it because the person you love hasn't said it.

This also pertains to your teachers. There will always be that negative teacher who will try to discourage you from being the best that you can be—and I've met my fair share of them. But then there are those teachers who empower you, who really live up to the concept of what being a teacher should be. If your teacher says you won't amount to anything, that will have an effect on you, because those words are coming from someone you respect, whose opinion you value. You can either live up to everything he says about you or you can try to prove him wrong. I have proven lots of my teachers wrong.

If you believe any of the negative things people say about you—and I mean the bitter, condescending comments that are not helpful in any way—then you have to question how much you love yourself.

Whenever someone says a negative thing about you that isn't connected to love—because sometimes people say negative things in order to motivate you that may appear to be negative but actually come out of love—I want you to make the decision to fall in love with who you are. Do not believe all the negative things that make you feel less than you are or cause you to doubt your abilities. I want you to flush what they say down the toilet and begin your own little mission to prove them wrong.

Even the things you say out loud can affect your mind-set. There is power in the tongue, and your energy will live up to the words you speak. The more you keep *saying* you're negative and depressed, the more your spirit and your body will try and live up to those words. People who say positive things all day, every day are more than likely going to have great energy.

When you say the word "depressed" you're giving your body and spirit permission to take you to a negative place. When you use the word "depressed," your spirit is going to try and live up to whatever that word is, and you normally associate the word "depressed" with someone being in their darkest state. When you say *I'm depressed*, a signal goes through your body—there's an energy that is activated in your mind—and it trickles throughout your body and brings you down to your lowest state.

As far as I'm concerned I've never truly been depressed in my life and I think this is because I don't *allow* myself to even say the word. I never use the word "depressed" freely and I always trip when I hear people say it. It's not that I don't believe that the spirit of being depressed doesn't exist, I've just never known it to exist in my own life. I could only imagine being depressed in relation to shooting a movie and preparing for a scene. For example, if I were going to be filming a death scene and the director starts to explain to me what my energy for the scene should be like, what I should be thinking about and how much the person who is going to die in the scene means to my character, he is planting dark, negative, and depressing seeds about how distraught I am supposed to be before I come to work the next day to film. The word "depressed" will activate the darkest state of my mind, and the rest of my body will be affected by those negative thoughts. I will tap into the spirit of being depressed to prepare for that scene and will become depressed because I will be living up to the thoughts I'm pounding into my mind.

So I never allow myself to *think* those words. We have to remove "depressed" from our vocabulary. Say *Rest in peace* to the word "depressed." Let's have a burial service for it because it has to go. You can be irritated, bothered, and annoyed with things in your life, but the word "depressed" has to be removed from your vocabulary because your spirit will live up to that word. I've had a negative mind-set, but when you use the word "depressed" it takes you over, so we have to put it in a coffin.

If you feel yourself going there, say to yourself *I'm happy!* and remind yourself of the good things in your life. If you keep saying that, your energy is going to reflect what happy is.

Reprogramming your mind is not as simple as saying *I'm happy* but being *aware* of how you say things will affect your mind-set and help rid you of your negative spirit.

Every Lesson Is a Blessing

Instead of focusing on the negatives like most people, I try my best to turn every negative into a positive, because like I said, it's all mental. It's important to think of every trial and tribulation as an opportunity, no matter how bad they may seem on the outside. Everything in life has the potential to affect you, and how you let your experiences affect you is up to you. I want you to look at your negative experiences as something that makes you stronger, not weaker. If you recognize how you learn from your actions—or how someone treated you—then the experience wasn't altogether negative.

People have said to me, "Tyrese, it's amazing how well you did for yourself, considering all the family problems you had as a kid." I did have huge obstacles to overcome, but now I look at the situation from a different angle: Would my life have been better if I didn't have the childhood I did? I'm not sure. I think it would have sent my life in a totally different direction. It's up to *me*, as a grown man, to decide how I let my childhood choices affect me and my decisions about how I'm going to live my life. I try to turn the negative things that happened to me into a positive learning experience for myself as a father and as a man. Do I slip up? Do negative thoughts creep into my mind? Are my actions sometimes negative? Do I sometimes have negative things to say about people? Do negative situations pop up that I don't just get over right away? Yes—that's what makes me human. But for the most part I try my best to look for the positive in every situation and continue on my mission to get out of my own way.

Sure, I still have regrets about things I've done in the past, but I make the effort to not sit on the pity potty I told you about earlier, because it will get me nowhere. My power is within what I know. I know that I made the choices I made because they were right for me at the time. I regret doing some of the things that I did, but I only regret them because I wasn't fully aware of the effect my actions had on people. But once I was educated and made aware of what I was doing and how I was impacting people, I made sure to change. In order to fix a problem, you first have to be *aware* of it.

I've learned to accept my actions because I know that every choice and decision I've ever made was part of God's plan. All I can do as a man and a human being is learn from them and grow. In a way, my bad choices led to my transformation and my getting to a better, more positive place in my life. That is why I believe that every lesson is a blessing.

Get Back to Self-Love: It's Okay to Be Selfish!

I've been asking you to think about how much you love yourself because it's essential if you want to maximize the blessings in your life. One way you can reprogram your mind and spirit is by getting back to self-love.

Self-love is the cure to self-hate. A key part of this is taking a break and doing something you love to do. I want you to get back to the things you used to enjoy because those activities will put you in a better mind-set so you can keep striving for more.

Try to focus on yourself for a change. In other words, I want you to be more selfish. Normally the word "selfish" is a negative because we were all raised to believe that being selfish is wrong, but I want to redefine it for you. The word "selfish" starts with "self." You have to be selfish and love yourself because you can't love anyone if you don't love yourself first. A good example of this, to put things in perspective, is what we are told to do in case of an airplane emergency. At the beginning of every flight, a flight attendant will usually go through various safety procedures. She will tell you that in the event of an emergency, oxygen masks will drop down and that all passengers should put on their own oxygen mask before helping others—even children. If your spouse or child is passed out, why wouldn't you help them first? Because if you don't help yourself first—if you don't get air into your own lungs—you won't be able to save anyone else. Use this situation as an example for how to deal with everyday life. Try putting yourself first for a change.

Why have you stopped yourself from doing the things that you love to do? Have you been too busy to love yourself? Do you make time for everyone else but not for easing your own suffering? Whether it's because of kids, work, your marriage, or friendships, many different things get in the way of finding time for yourself, but it's important to *make time* to do what you love, because it puts you in a positive frame of mind. It did something for you to read a book. It did something for you to go skating or bike riding in the park. You used to do it because it made you feel good. So why have you allowed the pressures and the circumstances of your life to take you away from the things that you used to love and enjoy doing? Doing these things will remind you of the positive things in your life. You have to love yourself enough to keep on doing what you're doing to get to the next level, to that better place you imagine for your life.

Many of us have totally gotten away from what we used to enjoy. We let our kids, boyfriends, wives, partners, jobs— anything—take us away from what we love to do. As you meet new people who come into your life, some will discourage you and try to stop you from being who you're ultimately destined to be or doing the things you used to love to do because they're not as into it. You need to find your own direction, be your own person, and not be ashamed of who you are, what you enjoy doing, or what you want to become. Get back to the things you enjoy. There's a selfishness about treating yourself well that has nothing to do with anyone else. It's just for you. Doing these things and taking time for yourself may remind you of the person you want to become.

There was a point in my life when I wasn't being selfish enough and I was suffering for it. When I was younger and making money for the first time, I felt very uncomfortable about having more than my family and the friends I grew up with. Because I wanted to keep it real I found myself doing a lot of things that I didn't really want to do but felt like I needed to in order to keep people thinking of me the way I *wanted* them to think of me. I wanted people to believe that I hadn't changed because of the amount of money I was making, the kind of car I was driving, my clothes, my jewelry, all of the fame and success, or all the attention I was getting from women. In my mind I wanted everybody to believe that I was still the same and I wasn't willing to spare any expense to do so.

I ended up giving away a lot of my money and helping people with their problems and personal issues that had nothing to do with me. I found myself trying to save a lot of people and doing things that put me in a more negative mind-set. Eventually, I got to a point where I was more comfortable in my own skin and I realized that I was really dealing with the adolescent pressures of trying to fit in. I think my biggest fear was that people would spread all my personal business and say negative things about me everywhere they went. My breaking point was when I experienced this from some family and friends. I realized that if it's in their character to talk shit about you or eat your reputation alive and spread negative stories about you everywhere they go, it doesn't matter if you were there for them or had their back or tried to prove them wrong—they're going to do it whether you helped them out or not. This realization liberated me from feeling obligated. I decided to shut down the ATM and end the feeding frenzy. If it's something they're going to do, they will do it whether you hold them down or not.

I realized much later that I had to get comfortable and not care what most people said about me, because I wasn't really helping them by giving them gifts. But I didn't feel that way in the beginning, or for a long time. I needed to be more selfish and not let people take advantage of my guilt or my generosity. I'm still very much affected by the things I see, and so I needed to become more selfish and try to stay away from many people's problems, negativity, and drama. I needed to distance myself a bit and to focus on my career so that I would not lose that part of me.

I don't want you to think that I'm telling you to abandon your loved ones and your responsibilities at home, work, or school. If you do that, you could be sabotaging your career, relationships, or future. Little acts of self-love are a good way to start loving yourself again. They will carry you through the difficult times and help you get out of the mind-set of being a victim. They will help you flush the pity potty. You will have a better mind-set so you can continue on the mission to that better place in your life.

Self-love reciprocates—it starts a whole new positive cycle—because love and positivity are powerful things. Self-love is the opposite of negativity and dysfunction. When you are more positive, you will most likely inspire good energy in your friends and family who care about you. If you love yourself, you will be able to identify the negative people in your life who are doing you wrong. It will help you get out of your own way because you'll be able to identify the negativity faster and clearer than before and stay away from it. We are responsible for who we are. If we don't do things that need to be done, we're just keeping ourselves in a spiritual and mental prison.

You Look the Way You Think of Yourself

I've explained that the body is a slave of the mind and whatever mind-set you have and how much you love yourself will affect everything you do. I'm going to take this idea to the next level: You *look* the way you think of yourself.

Just like the phrase *You are what you eat*, if you're miserable internally, your body is going to look exactly like how you feel because what you look like on the outside is a direct reflection of your spirit.

Your confidence and your aura are all a result of your mental state. You look and carry yourself the way you think of yourself. It starts with your mind and then works its way down into your body.

You won't have to tell people if you're depressed or happy. You don't have to explain to people how you feel about yourself, you just have to walk into the room and most people are going to see it. You don't have to shout *Hey, guys, I'm happy!* People will see it because your energy will reveal it to them. Your friends, family, and most people you meet can tell that something is wrong. If you have a negative spirit you can still have a nice and bright smile, but that only means that you have great toothpaste. Your loved ones can still see the pain in your smile. Can't *you* tell when your own friends are going through pain and dysfunction? I've met a few people who have gone through some serious drama and life-threatening situations who were able to put on their game face and hide it, but I have found that most people show what they're going through without even realizing it.

In my own mind, I often question people who have over-the-top, super-hyper, and big personalities; sometimes, I can't stop from wondering what's really going on or what they are covering up by having such a big personality. Just because you're the loudest, most hyper person in the club doesn't mean you're happy. Just because you're driving the most expensive car doesn't mean you have gas money. It becomes a game of perception versus reality; we tend to make decisions about who people are, what they're going through, and whatever else based on the way people *appear* to be.

Some people dress trashy or sloppy. Some people are big and weigh a lot—but I'm not telling you to be a size two. There are some people who may be heavier than others and they have a great spirit; they are completely happy and content and very comfortable with the reality of their size, and I respect that. Being smaller doesn't necessarily mean that you're happier. Some people have health issues they can't control, but if you are overweight because you have *purposely* stopped trying to turn it around, your body will represent exactly what you're thinking.

Your body is a slave of your mind, so *you* are the reason you are out of shape. I'm speaking from my own experience here. A few years ago, I let myself go a bit. I weighed almost two hundred and fifty pounds. I was eating my life away, and it was no one's fault but mine. I used to be that guy saying I didn't care, with the excuse that living in the moment was all that mattered. I would buy XXXL T-shirts to cover up who I was becoming. Without realizing, I was dealing with self-sabotage and self-defeat. I didn't realize that I was becoming too complacent until someone said to me, "When you walk in a room, Tyrese, you look like you don't give a fuck. You don't have to explain anything to anybody." I'll talk more about becoming complacent later, but please know that I'm coming from a real place. I was there. The food became more important than maintaining the blessings that I got from being in shape. Eating everything in sight became more important than me and my career.

You are the one who chose to eat a cheeseburger instead of a salad, not anyone else. Why are you not taking care of yourself? Why don't you feel you deserve better? How much do you love yourself? I didn't get my first Guess contract by showing up with love handles and a gut. I got it because I went to the gym and gave a damn. Rewards come to those who love themselves, and it's really hard to say you love yourself when you look like you don't care. Well, we all get lazy sometimes and need that kick in the backside to get motivated. If you can find time to eat, you can find time to work out. Every day you make it a point to eat because you get hungry. Get back to self-love. Make it a point to start exercising in any way you can, and start eating right—you'll see the results.

Some people have said to me that they would work out, but they aren't motivated enough to work out alone and don't have money for a trainer. In response to that I tell them—and I'll tell you—don't allow your pride and your ego to stop you from befriending someone who is in better shape than you. Go to the gym and find somebody who is in great shape. This person doesn't have to be a trainer; he or she can just be somebody you see in the gym every day around the same time. They should be in much better shape than you. Tell them that you want to work out with them because their body looks the way you want your body to look. Just ask questions, and they will give you information. From my experience, most people that are in shape normally have a lot of confidence and are excited to share what they know, because ultimately if people are asking them questions about how to get in shape it's most likely because they look good and others have noticed. They'll tell you about the weights you should use, or show you different machines. You can ask them about the foods they're eating or not eating. You can even say to them, "Pay me no mind, you don't have to train me, but I'm going to come here, and I'm just so inspired by you, I'm going to work out next to you and do the things that you do, I hope you don't mind." If they agree, that's even better. All of that is free: free training and free motivation. This way, you can end up working out with somebody for free and have somebody to keep you inspired. The only expense you have is the gym membership, which you should have already.

If you want to get in shape, you should also consider whom you're hanging out with. If everybody around you is eating bad foods, that's what you're going to eat because that's the spirit you're in. We usually spend time with people who do the same things we do, who have the same interests. If you want to change your body, your friends and family may make you feel uncomfortable about going to the gym or eating healthier if that's not what they're into. It's like oil and water: There's no way that oil could ever get along with water. If your friends are eating tons of greasy foods and you're trying to stay away from that, you may have to stay away from them.

It's all part of a cycle. As you reprogram your mind to get rid of the negative spirit you'll feel better and look better. You create the reality you want for your life, and taking care of your body will only help you love yourself more.

Your Home Reflects Your Spirit

You are a direct reflection of your thoughts and spirit, and that includes the way you live because your home is an extension of you. So if you look the way you think of yourself, the same goes for your house, your car, and all your personal possessions.

When you walk into somebody's house, you're technically walking inside of that person's thoughts. You're seeing their idea of how they view themselves. If your house or room is dirty and smells like shit, then that says a lot about what you think of yourself.

Some people claim they would take better care of their car if it were nicer or more expensive, but they *don't* have a more expensive car. You should take better care of what you have, no matter how much it costs. Everything has value especially if it's yours, if you worked hard to earn the money to pay for it. I've been in some really nice houses in the hood that are clean and have nicely mowed front yard lines. Some of the people who live in these homes may be struggling financially, but they think better of themselves and are making the best of their bad circumstances. They value their possessions and treat them well. At the end of the day, it's the mind-set of the people living in the house that creates the mess. A person's location could change, but if their mind-set stays the same, so will the results. It doesn't matter what your point of navigation is, what city, state, or country you move to; if you've got ghetto or dysfunctional or dirty habits, they're going to follow you wherever you are. You can take folks out of the hood but you can't take the hood out of them. If you bring your drama and your negativity to a beautiful new house, it will look more disgusting than some of the worst homes in Watts.

Some of your homes are nasty. I want you to clean your house, your car, your workspace, or any other place you spend time. Clearing the clutter and getting rid of the garbage is a physical way to rid yourself of your negative spirit. If your stove is black, if you have dishes piled on top of each other in the sink, if you haven't cleaned out your closet or opened your blinds in years, if it's been too long since you washed your car and you've got garbage strewn everywhere, then you must not think you deserve anything nice in your life. Why won't you clean your home because you value it and *want* to keep it nice?

Now, it's possible that you have a more positive spirit and you're just messy. This may be a reflection of your childhood environment because who we are as adults is somehow connected to who we were as kids. You should decide if you want to break the messy habits that the person who raised you may have instilled in you.

This is a note for you parents out there: Don't assume your kids are too young to be affected by your choices. The way you live, how clean you keep your home, the men and women you invite to be around will impact your children. It's real easy to assume that because they're young they don't know what's happening, but they do. You're planting seeds early in their life, telling them that it's okay to live in filth. Most adults have a bad habit of living their lives by the idea of *Do as I say, not as I do*, but kids just learn to *do* even if it seems like they don't pay attention to what you say.

Let me be clear: I want to activate self-love for *you* instead of doing these things and making adjustments for other people. You have to want to do these things on your own behalf. You represent your thoughts. Why did you decide to clean your place before company came over, when that wasn't the way your place was at first? Stop performing. Do it when no one is looking. Clean up your space and do it for you.

You create the reality you want for yourself. If you want to love yourself more, you've got to take care of the home front. Clean up a little bit and when you do, it will make such a big difference in your life, environment, and spirit—I promise you.

What Is Your Bottom Line?

Once you've started to reprogram your mind, you can set your bottom line without any of the negativity clouding your judgment. You can figure out what you want for yourself and how you want to be treated in a clearer way. It's important to set a bottom line because it will help you control how much dysfunction and negativity you allow into your life.

A bottom line is a personal boundary that you will not allow yourself or other people in your life to cross. If you're complaining about your life, ask yourself, *What is my bottom line?* If you don't have one, someone will always cross it and if you don't love yourself enough, you're going to let them do it. If you love yourself enough to know what your bottom line is, you're going to have a clearer picture of what you're willing to tolerate and how you want to be treated.

My motivation to work hard and want more for myself came from my lowest point, when I said, *I'm done with being broke and hungry. Done with this lifestyle, being in the hood, putting my life on the line every day. This ain't it. I'm disgusted with the whole situation.* Looking back on it, I can see that I was establishing a bottom line that I knew I could never cross again. Even though I did have some good times in the hood, what made it so easy to draw my bottom line was everything else that came with living there. There are things about the hood that I had no control over, especially as a kid. So I made my choice, and I had to get out. I wanted better and recognized that if I really had a problem with my life, then I had to do something.

You can set a bottom line for anything in your life, but it should always be in relation to how much you love yourself and how much you want for yourself. Set yourself up to be happier than you are now. How much are you willing to tolerate?

Everyone's bottom line is different. We've all been exposed to different experiences, so our tolerance for certain situations will vary from person to person. Only you can answer the question for yourself. What is the line that you refuse to cross?

In order to answer this question truthfully, you should try to think of the most challenging situations of your life. Figure out which experiences were necessary and helped you grow, and which ones caused you nothing but grief, drama, stress, and heartache.

Everyone has relationship issues. People are always going to argue. But what is your bottom line? Is it your partner disrespecting you—or worse? If you don't stick to your bottom line, you're not showing yourself the respect or self-love you deserve—and other people will walk all over you. If you had known what your bottom line was, you would be more aware of your personal boundaries. Whether you have tough skin or not, everyone should have a bottom line.

From this point forward, I want you to keep an eye out for any new dysfunction that tries to work its way into your life and bottom-line it right away. Perhaps you're spending too much money, or not spending *enough* time with your family. Maybe you're not going to church, or a friend or coworker is taking advantage of you. Whatever it is, relate that particular scenario to your new bottom line, and react accordingly. Don't allow friends or family to redefine your bottom line, because they are not the ones who have to live with the consequences.

I can sometimes make people uncomfortable with my bottom line now because I know what I'm willing to put up with. When you have a bottom line, you don't have to open yourself up to have a conversation about it. You don't need to announce what your bottom line is; it's something people could just experience when you set your own standards. Are you always going to be a pushover, someone who lies there while others drive over you?

For a very long time I was uncomfortable telling people what I was really feeling and thinking, because I was afraid they would judge me. Even if I was in a room with five or six people and wanted to have a one-on-one private meeting I felt too uncomfortable making the simple request that others step out of the room. I was so self-conscious that people would think negatively about me and I ended up being the victim in my own environment. If you're not comfortable in your own skin, or not bold enough in your truth, you will always be on the receiving end of everybody's personalities.

I decided forever ago to not be a pushover. I now live by the words "You should always expect the things that you accept." This applies to both people and situations. Meaning, if you accept that somebody treats you or talks to you in a disrespectful way, then you should always *expect* them to keep doing it. But if you nip that in the bud, they won't do it anymore because you will have established your bottom line and clearly made it unacceptable for them to treat you that way again. I decided that I would no longer accept certain behavior. My environment is so much more comfortable now because I am able to control it.

You have to understand yourself and the situations you find yourself in, and ask yourself if they fit with your goals and what you want for yourself. If they're not, then consider what your bottom line is. How much are you willing to put up with? Whatever it is, is it worth it? Is the outcome going to justify your struggle? Will the ends justify the means? Only you can answer that question, and if the answer is no, then stop complaining about it and start fixing it.

Once you set your bottom line, try to never waver from it. You'll be able to see things so much clearer and you'll be more in control. If you love yourself enough, then everything and everyone will come into perspective. Your bottom line will help keep out the negative spirit.

You Are Pregnant with the New You

I've been prompting you to make a choice. That choice is *you*. Do you love yourself enough to want better? You may have a lot of challenges in your life right now and it can be scary to realize that you have a lot to fix and a lot to change. You may not love yourself enough *yet* but I know you can get there. You're in the middle of a war, going through all this stuff, but you can't give up! Let me share something with you that my mentor John Bryant said to me once: *You're pregnant with the new you.*

Now, it might sound strange, but he was right. He told me this seven or eight years ago when I was going through some difficult growing pains in business and in my personal life. I was in Philly for a show and had a bunch of interviews and in-store autograph signings lined up. I was miserable because I had a lot going on, and I was complaining because I was exhausted. After listening to me for an hour, John said, "Tyrese, are you done?" When I said yes, he told me, "You know what you're going through right now? You're pregnant."

"What do you mean, I'm pregnant? I'm not pregnant!"

"You're pregnant with the new you." He explained that just like any mother who is pregnant, there are cramps, there are complications, there's discomfort. I had something growing inside me and like women who are pregnant I didn't anticipate all the issues that arise when you make significant changes in your life.

And then he told me that having an abortion of the new

me was not an option. What John told me that day has stayed with me ever since and I think about it when I'm going through a tough time, because I see every lesson as a blessing. What he told me made me realize that everything I was going through in my life was for a *reason*: I was working on my career and my life, on my way to becoming the man I wanted to be.

I want you to love yourself more because I want you to go out and accomplish everything you have ever wanted for yourself. I want you to want more for yourself. There is nothing I've been able to accomplish that you can't. But you just have to try!

I want to encourage you to get back into the things you loved to do, and further educate yourselves on the things you're passionate about. I know that kids, weight gain, marriage, divorce, and life's responsibilities can distract you from the goals you've always wanted to accomplish. If you got off track, remember that the track is still there. Respark your mission, get back on that track, and get it going.

You have to reprogram your spirit so that you can get to that *better place* you know you deserve. Remember, it's all about the hustle. Don't stay at home waiting for the opportunities to knock at your door. I decided I loved myself and you can, too. You have the power and you have more to offer than you imagine. You just have to believe it.

Chapter 3

Are You the Master of Your Environment?

Are you the master of your environment? The simple answer is YES, we all are. As the master of your environment *you* are responsible for the reality you create in life, relationships, work, and school. You are responsible for how people perceive you.

The question is, *What kind* of master are you? *How* are you controlling your environment? What kind of control do you have? Are you acting with enough self-love and positive energy? As I said earlier, what you do with your life is a direct reflection of how you feel about yourself. If you love yourself better, you are going to *want* better. Once you get rid of the negative spirit, you will be more capable of controlling your environment because you'll know your actions are coming from a more positive place.

I hope to make you more aware of your actions and *how* you control your environment. Sometimes we're not fully in control and allow other factors to affect the kind of master we are. You may not *own* your actions and may be acting on a subconscious level, and that will prevent you from succeeding and becoming a true master of your environment. I struggled with this even after I became successful.

At different times in our life we all need a wake-up call to open our eyes and understand our actions. Let me tell you how I learned this myself.

Becoming the Master of Your Environment: What Kind of Master Are You?

I have always sought advice from people I admired and wanted to be more like. Seeking guidance, hustling, and reaching out have served me well in life. Sometimes people give you advice that really opens your eyes and shows you *how* you need to change. Will Smith did that for me. I had to become a better master of my environment and take control of my identity but in order to even *know* I had to do that, I had to hear some of the worst things about myself from one of the biggest stars in Hollywood.

Like Angie, Mr. Charlie, Gayle Atkins, and Reggie Andrews, Will Smith opened my eyes and showed me a better version of what I could be. When I first started talking with Will, I was almost thirty, I was married, and I had a baby girl, Shayla. I was still working hard, but until I hooked up with Will, I had no idea that I was on the path to destroying my career.

I had started my career in music but I was lucky enough to get into films. Hollywood and the music industry are different worlds, with different kinds of responsibilities. In a way, recording artists are allowed to be more arrogant and egotistical and get away with it because everything is solely about them and for them. When you're a recording artist, it's about your video, it's about your singing. You're not always working on a project like "We Are the World," where there are forty different people performing on the track. Movies and music are two different realities, so when you're coming from that mind-set like I was, where it's normally all about you and doing your thing, you become desensitized to the fact that the things you say and do have an effect on your work environment and the people you work with. You are the sun, and everything else revolves around you.

Once I had broken into films, I felt like I had made it: I was making a lot of money, the phone was still ringing, and when I went onstage to perform, everybody was still screaming my name. I was too comfortable, I was starring in movies—it was all still happening.

But I was lazy and complacent. I wasn't working to maintain the blessings. I had put on a load of weight before I filmed *Waist Deep* but I didn't do anything about it. I was the star of the film, I was number one on the call sheet, but I was as big as a house, eating my life away. I had gotten to a point where I didn't care about the way the world saw me. I felt big, I didn't like the way I felt, but there was something in me that didn't stop me from eating or sabotaging my life. I was not fully aware of what I was doing to myself and my career.

Most of you who have seen the movie *Waist Deep* are probably thinking, *What the hell are you talking about, Tyrese? You looked just fine.* But I know I could have been in better shape. And when you know it, it doesn't really matter what anybody else feels. It's about *you* knowing that you weren't at your best. I should have been forty pounds lighter, shredded, in shape, and looking to take advantage of every opportunity that came from starring in a movie, while looking my best. That wasn't my best.

I was around two hundred and fifty pounds, and in the movie, the director wanted me to wear a tank top in a scene where I would be running up a street, chasing a car that was driving away with my son. When I was on set and we were filming that scene, I couldn't help but think about Will Smith's amazing scene in *Bad Boys*, where he's running with his shirt open, shooting his gun as cars explode all around him. That particular shot right there was a huge action moment and one of the scenes that made Will Smith the A-list star that he is, because it was just so well done. So while we were filming *Waist Deep* I was thinking a lot about that scene. I knew I didn't *quite* look as good as I should have. In *Bad Boys*, Will Smith was acting like he was tired at the end of the scene, but I was *really* tired as I ran up the street, because I was just so big. Still, I didn't do anything about it because no matter how bad I looked, checks were still getting cut, people were still calling and wanting me to be in their movies. I've learned that in Hollywood there is no sense of consequence.

On the set of a couple of movies that I shot a few months later, I was not really owning the craft or taking it seriously. I was lazy and unprofessional and wasn't on point. I was showing up late sometimes to the set, talking on my Sidekick during filming, and I was totally out of shape and didn't care that I was out of shape. I was too loud, cracking jokes while other people were trying to get in character and focus on their scenes. These were career-making movies, so what the hell was I doing? If anybody had just said to me *Tyrese, what you're doing is wrong*, then it would have stopped, but no one ever said anything, because in Hollywood, not many people are willing to say how they really feel because they're afraid of getting fired. The mind-set is, *Don't piss off the stars*, so I was on these film sets and people were talking about me, complaining about my behavior, and I didn't know it. I was destroying my reputation and nobody was saying anything to me about it.

I didn't realize anything was wrong until I met up with Will Smith. I had always liked to seek advice and I knew I needed some great advice at that point. I had sensed something was wrong but I wasn't fully sure what it was. I told Charlie Mack, a mutual friend of ours, that I wanted to set up a time to chop it up with Will, and Charlie made it happen. He had known Will for about thirty years and through him I had run into Will many times, but this particular moment and this conversation we had shook me up—it was like my whole world caved in.

Will and I talked for hours—about three or four hours in a row. As I spoke my truth and put it all on the table, going into detail about how I was acting, what people were saying, what I was doing, Will just kept breaking it all down, dropping advice on me, painting the picture of how I was messing up and explaining why I had been getting the kind of responses I was getting.

It was only when I had this conversation with Will that it was made so clear to me that it was *me*, that with my attitude *I* was the one who had planted those negative seeds. Will made me aware that I shouldn't have been complaining about press issues when I was not able to say that I was the best version of me in these movies. He told me, *You weren't the best version of Tyrese, so none of that matters*. I was showing up on set with top-notch directors, much heavier than I could have been, so what was I thinking? No matter what level you get to in your life and career you can always do better, so you have to stay sharp.

I probably got up from the table about ten times during the course of the conversation, screaming, "I never thought about it like that!" I was really tripping about the things he was saying to me and the way he was breaking it down and making it so clear to me that I had been killing my career. If I hadn't had that conversation with Will, then my outlook and my focus and the way I've been doing things would have totally killed me, and no one would have said anything. They would have just sat back and watched me do it.

Will explained that in any professional environment, and especially in Hollywood, it's all about survival. He said—and I'm paraphrasing here—"Tyrese, let me explain something: Everyone that works on a movie set is on one mission and one mission only: to feed their families. That's what they want to do. They may love what they do but they show up every single day and work their asses off to feed their families. Nobody's going through all of that for no reason. So technically speaking, when you're showing up lazy, out of shape, and unfocused, you have decided that you don't care if people feed their families. And when you get in the way of someone feeding their families, they're going to get in the way of you feeding your family."

Will understood that I had grown up in the music industry. He had to spell it out that when you're in movies, everything you do, your behavior, and your flaws, affects everybody involved with a film. When you get on a movie set, especially in Hollywood, the main focus tends to be the producers, the director, the stars—the "important" folks, so to speak—but after speaking to Will, I realized the value in everyone else who's on the set. I was not going to be the reason on any level that anyone on a movie set couldn't feed their family. I wasn't going to do that. And that's where it all changed.

It was like a train crashed into me because I literally started *seeing* most of the things Will made me aware of. I understood how I had affected people's reactions to me. I was not proud of it. I really hate working backward, I hated knowing that I had pissed people off and now had to fix things, which is so much harder than getting it right the first time. But knowing what I know, I've got to get it right the first time.

Will also told me about what happened when he watched *Waist Deep* with his wife, Jada. They were at home, and Will was enjoying some ice cream. When they got to the scene where I was running up the street in that tank top—the scene that to me had been an homage to *Bad Boys*—Jada looked at Will, he looked at her, she looked down at the ice cream and then looked back up at him. Will got up, put down the ice cream, paused the movie, and went and ran five miles. When Will told me that, *I* got up from the table and screamed. I had him in mind when I shot that scene, remembering how cool Will looked in *Bad Boys*...and Will had watched *Waist Deep* and was so disgusted at how big I was that he went and ran five miles to make sure that he never let himself go like I had. He laughed so hard when I told him, but that was a humbling moment for me.

That one conversation really created the *beast* in me. Will's advice and the information he gave me *completely* changed my outlook on life. He educated me on the way other people see things and our conversation made me change everything that

I was doing. That night he also told me something that became central to my life—that you can often tell how far your life and career will go based on the five people you spend the most time with—and we'll discuss that in depth later.

I wasn't only impacted by what Will said because of how my actions had affected or bothered other people. I was impacted because I had a new bottom line: my daughter. I was not going to kill my career and I was going to do anything I needed to do, because I wasn't willing to tell my daughter that I could not give her the life or education she deserved. There was no way I was going to do that.

The fact that I now knew these things elevated me to a whole other level. At that point I could no longer say I didn't know any better. I had to take control of my identity. I was the master of my environment but as a master I needed an overhaul.

You Control Your Identity

Until you have a conversation with a person who can really make you aware of what you're doing wrong—the way you're acting, how you're coming off and affecting people with what you're doing—most people like me will have no clue. You're just showing up and you're just being whoever you are. Most people don't want to know the truth about their actions, but you've got to welcome it. Even if there's not an actual altercation or confrontation that makes people tell you the truth you have to *ask* them, *Will you be honest with me? Is there anything that you want to make me aware of? Is there anything you think I should be doing differently from what I'm doing?* Most people will tell you you're fine and you can only hope they're really saying what's on their mind, but at least you planted the seed that you're *welcoming* the truth. You should make every effort to find people who will tell you the truth. When you've got people in your circle who believe in you, they will be willing to tell you the truth.

I saw the error of my ways and took control of my image and my identity. I worked hard to change the way people think of me, and it all happened from that conversation with Will. You can either run around complaining, bitching and moaning, and blaming other people for what's going wrong, or you can decide to hear the truth and get in front of it.

I laced up my boots and got out there and started making changes right away. I was with Will on the set of one of his movies, training with him, running five miles a day. My diet was so strict it was crazy, my focus and level of execution was on a whole other level. I started seeing the effects of my changes with my own eyes.

The effort wasn't just about showing goodwill toward the people I worked with; it was also about getting in front of my image and how people perceived me. I controlled my body and got in shape and began to control the reality of my life.

When I arrived on the set of my next movie, I made sure that my professionalism, my focus, and my level of execution were the complete opposite of what they had been before. I was on a different level. I was training on set every day and there was all this great energy. It was like no one recognized me. Everyone called Will to tell him what a great difference he had made, because they knew he had taken me under his wing and was mentoring me.

Take control of your identity. You have more control of the way people think of you than you would like to believe. What do you want people to think of you? You are the master of your environment and *you* create the reality of whatever you want people to think of you. You have to be aware of how you create that perception because people respond to what they see, whether it's how you look or how you act.

Even though my conversation with Will was specifically about Hollywood, his advice was viral; I took that information and used it in my music career and in other parts of my life. People are just trying to feed their families, so *show up*. What you're doing in this world has an effect on people and the outcome of their survival and *your* survival. You may be the master of your environment but *how* are you affecting other people's environments? What kind of environment are you creating?

I became incredibly conscious of how I was running my business. I have never limited myself to what I know or what I'm comfortable with and if I had allowed my ego to convince me that I knew it all, I would have killed everything I was trying to grow. I never make anybody who works with me feel uncomfortable about telling me the truth. I consider my business a ship and I have to keep it afloat. If your ship is about to go down like the *Titanic*, you have to ask, *What type of ship is the captain running? Does he make the people who work on his ship uncomfortable with telling him something that he* needs *to know?* If we're about to hit an iceberg and none of my employees is willing to come up here and give me that valuable piece of information because they think it's going to be a reflection of their incompetence and that they are going to get fired, then we're really going to drown. You may have dropped the ball and made a mistake, but if you're uncomfortable or afraid of making your boss aware of something that's going wrong, we're all going down, because no one will know they have to fix it. I have tried to create an environment in my office where I want everyone to feel comfortable telling me the truth so we can maintain the blessings of keeping the Tyrese ship—which includes everybody in my life and everybody in their lives—on board. We can all survive, we can all keep eating, we can all flourish and keep it together.

I am really close to an entertainer whose business was going down like the *Titanic*. On one pivotal night, he discovered that one of his productions had not been properly marketed or promoted, so the show wasn't sold out. He was especially pissed that his people told him this on the day *of* the show. The same night he found out, we were sitting in his dressing room and he told me how he would have fixed it. He said, "All they had to do was tell me that the show wasn't sold out. I would have canceled it or come into town three or four days earlier to do some radio, or had the promoter spend more marketing money to amp up awareness of the show." I had to pick the right time to say this to him, but I was thinking that more than likely his people were afraid of him, which is why they never said anything. I love this guy but I also knew his reputation: He was known for firing people and making his employees feel uncomfortable, and in these trying times, no one wants to be out of a job. I set him down and said, "You may want to consider that you're making the people on your team uncomfortable with telling you the truth about everything that is going on with your business." He heard what I was saying and took it to heart.

Soon after, he took his entire staff of thirty out to dinner and let the drinks flow. He got them a little drunk so that they would feel comfortable enough to tell him what they were *really* thinking and feeling. He told them he loved them and that he wasn't going to fire any of them *but* that they needed to start telling him what was really going on. Some people really unleashed on him and let him have it and other people were more reserved, but he learned so much and the conversation completely changed the dynamics of his business. He called me a week later to make me aware that I had inspired him to speak with his staff. From that point on, his productions continued to sell out. Hearing the truth, opening up their communication, and being open to honesty made all the difference in the world for his business. Remember: The worst boss is a *blind boss* who is unaware of most of the important inner dealings of his or her business.

Some people would be better off blind because they don't want to see the reality of life. That's not me. Will opened my eyes and showed me the truth of where I was. I want you to open your eyes and see that you *can* make changes and take things to another level. You are responsible for being the master of your environment and you can create a new perception of yourself and be a more *aware* master of your environment.

Breaking the Cycle: Are You a Master or a Monster?

I channeled everything that Will and I talked about, and the advice he gave me really shook up every aspect of my life. Most of the changes I made had to do with people I did business with. I understood how complacent I had been in my work and started to get in front of my professional image, but I also needed to look at my personal relationships. Will had given me the book called *As a Man Thinketh* by James Allen and reading it hit me like another train. As soon as I finished reading it, I ran eighteen miles. The title comes from the proverb, *As a man thinketh in his heart, so is he* and I knew I had to start looking at what was going on in my heart. My ex-wife and I were fighting a lot and I wanted clarity on everything I was going through at the time.

Just as our homes and how we look are a reflection of our thoughts and how much we love ourselves, we are a reflection of the environment we grew up in. To become better masters of our environment we have to *understand* our environment—the one we come from and the one we're currently in.

Most of us don't recognize that who we are as adults is directly connected to what we were exposed to as kids. We can't break the cycle and truly get in control of our environment if we're not conscious of the fact that we may be doing the same thing our mothers and fathers did.

I knew that I was a reflection of my environment: When I was younger, my environment had created the monster in me. After I started going to the private behavioral school, I had become more violent—fighting and acting crazy—compared to what I had been before. But once I left that school and went to Locke High School, I was minding my p's and q's. I wasn't the bad kid they had led me to believe. But I realized I wasn't only a reflection of the schools I attended. I was a reflection of my childhood as a whole.

Growing up, I had been exposed to images of verbal, physical, emotional, and spiritual abuse and condescending and vindictive arguments and behavior. If you grew up around negativity like that, you may find yourself duplicating what you were exposed to, or you can specifically decide to break the cycle and not be like that. A lot of us don't even know that what we're doing or thinking is wrong because these were the images that we were used to so it's not different or strange—it's *normal*. This is not meant to sound like an excuse for any of my actions. I had already broken one cycle—I don't drink or smoke because drugs and alcohol messed up my childhood—and once I read *As a Man Thinketh* I realized I had to break another negative cycle.

I used to be attracted to dysfunctional people. It wasn't something I was conscious or aware of. I discovered the pattern that, without my even knowing, if I was in a relationship, and my girlfriend didn't cry or get emotional or if she wasn't willing to argue, I figured she clearly did not love me. It was impossible for her to make me believe that she felt a certain way about me if she was not reacting to my pushing her buttons. I was connecting dysfunction to love because that's what I had been exposed to.

Growing up, the word "I" was never in front of the words "love you." I heard *Love you!* but nothing about the *actions* really represented the word "love," in my opinion. So I didn't know what I was supposed to do. How could I show real love when my interpretation of love throughout my childhood was dysfunctional?

I would think, *There is a problem but we don't know how to fix it.* There was something going on in my relationships that was unhealthy and dysfunctional but I didn't know what to say or what to do to make it better. *What is it in me?* That is a question I asked myself when I was with women who talked to me in a disrespectful, condescending, and evil tone that made me react and get angry. I would say to myself, *What part of me as a man made her feel comfortable talking to me that way? What do I say to make her stop talking to me this way? At what point in our relationship did she say I could talk to her any way that I wanted? What part of the game is this?* I was addicted to dysfunction, because I was dysfunctional. I just wasn't conscious of it.

Many people love dysfunction. They get challenged by it, they're intrigued by it, they love arguing, and it just *does* something for them and so they will create drama where there is none. I used to start arguments when things were too peaceful, just to argue, just to get back to that familiar feeling. I would ask myself, *Why am I arguing, why am I starting this?* But I couldn't help it.

It is very scary—and I am putting all the emphasis on it in the world—to be duplicating images and the actions from your childhood and the things you were exposed to and not even be conscious of it. There was a point when my ex-wife and I were arguing and I realized, *Oh my God, this is exactly what was happening twenty years ago.* When I saw our child reacting to how her mother and I were yelling, all of a sudden I could see what was going on. I couldn't assume she was too young to understand what was going on because I knew what was going on when I was younger. And the question was, Will she become acclimated to this? Will she just get used to it and think it's normal? If it becomes normal for her, when she starts dating, she'll begin to look for a duplicate of her father in her man and she will look for a guy who will scream and yell at her, because she will think that screaming and yelling during arguments is normal because that's what she grew up around.

I wasn't going to let that happen. I needed to break the cycle. I realized the pattern and I needed to reprogram myself, just like Locke High School deprogrammed me from thinking I had to fight like an animal. Just like one of my mom's ex-boyfriends reprogrammed her and made her realize that physical abuse in a relationship is not love.

I wanted to stay married for me and my ex-wife but as a father, I couldn't stay married because we were not getting along, and I saw how our child looked sad when she saw Mommy and Daddy arguing. I could tell that what we were doing was affecting her. Kids are not stupid. They know something is wrong when Mommy and Daddy get loud and come in all angry and mean. They're affected by it.

So, unfortunately, divorce was my form of breaking the cycle. I had set my bottom line, and it was our daughter. I did not want to create a new Gibson monster. I didn't want to create a monster in our child. I didn't want her to grow up acclimated to arguments, saying mean and evil things. I recognized the dysfunction in me, and I understood further *why* it existed in our relationship. I know how dysfunction impacted my life and my outlook on life and I didn't want those negative seeds planted in my child and the best way to fix it was to get away from it. I finally saw what was going on and I had to make a grown-up decision. I was actively deciding to change my family's history and that of the future Gibson generations.

After the marriage was over I wondered if my ex-wife and I would still be married if our daughter weren't in the picture. I kept thinking this because we had a bunch of unresolved issues before we got married and our being married only heightened the drama. But if our daughter weren't in the picture, those problems would have just been affecting my ex-wife and me, not us and our child.

We can create monsters in each other. And then once we create that monster, we want to run away from it, and that's what I did. I created a monster in my ex-wife and I couldn't handle what I created. She created a monster in me, and she couldn't handle what she had created. I remember what we used to be like together. We had a ball, but at the time, I didn't think I had it in me to stick around to get back to the way we used to be.

I had the time of my life with my ex-wife. We had the most fun of all the relationships I had ever been in. We laughed, we traveled, we joked, we were silly, we had a good time. But the problems were definitely there. When I pray, I just hope and pray that God heals her and removes any bitterness, hostility, or anger that she may have toward me, from all of the things that I may have done wrong. I pray for her all the time, that she's able to heal and get past the things that didn't work out between us, because I want her to be happy.

Sometimes I think it's crazy that people try and stay in each other's lives when they know the relationship is clearly dysfunctional. I'm not a coward. Divorce for me wasn't a cop-out; I'm not a quitter, I'm a realist. And my being a realist is still within my opinion and my reality. Everyone argues—it's normal, it happens. The question is, What level of dysfunction are your arguments reaching? *How* are you arguing? Ask yourself, are your arguments evil, vindictive, and malicious, or are you just having a disagreement? Our arguments were unhealthy, and that was the difference. What we were going through, and the *way* we were going through it, was just way too negative. And I decided it was enough.

Can You Break the Cycle?

A few years ago, I experienced a conversation that I will never forget. It messed me up and made me really think that my mentor John Bryant was right, that most of who we are as adults is someway, somehow directly connected to our childhood.

I was living at a friend's house in the Hollywood Hills while I was working on an album. One night I asked my mom to come out and visit me. We were sitting in the Jacuzzi of my friend's infinity-edge pool, so it seemed like we could slip off the side of the mountain. There was a full moon, and it was pitch-black in the hills, so other than a few lights that were on in individual houses the only light that my mother and I really had was from the moon.

It was one of those nights—my mother was sober and we were getting along, it was the first time we ever had relaxing mother-and-son time in a Jacuzzi. Something in me told me to ask about her childhood, which I had never done before. I asked her, "Mama, what was it like in your house with your mother?" This is when the night got spooky and really scary for me. She said, "Well, my mama was a complete drunk. She was so drunk all the time, like every day, all day. She would lose control of her bladder because she had so much alcohol in her system. She would bring these boyfriends to the house. I *hated* her boyfriends because she would let them come in, and they would just run the whole place. They would control everything as if we had no say-so, it was just crazy. She used to hit us and she was abusive and her boyfriends used to hit us, and they were abusive. I just felt like I had no control of my childhood."

While I was listening to her describe her mother's actions and other details that she shared that I won't reveal here, I was shocked that she was describing her *own* actions as my mom. I could have said the exact same words about *her*. But when she was telling me her story not even *once* did she connect herself, her habits, what she did, what she said, or the way she raised us, with what her own mother did to her or what she had been exposed to. I said to her, "Mama, you just messed me up right now."

And she said, "What?"

I looked her in her eyes and said, "So, Mama, I'm not in this Jacuzzi with my mother. I'm in this Jacuzzi with my grandmother."

She got loud and firm with me, and said, "What are you talking about?! I'm nothing like my mama." She got really pissed, and wanted to get out of the Jacuzzi. She was clearly shocked and distraught, disgusted even, that I had compared her to her own mother.

"Mama, yes you *are*. You were drunk all the time. You lost control of your bladder a few times and didn't even know it was happening. You put your boyfriends over us. Our house had dysfunction and fights and verbal and physical abuse. Everything you just described to me about your mother and the way she raised you and the things that she exposed you to are the same exact things I'm able to say about *you*. So I'm in the Jacuzzi with my grandmother."

I exhaled. It was as if she had taken the breath out of my

body by dropping this stuff on me. I said, "Mama, I want you to know I love you so much for sharing this with me, because I forgive you now. I forgive you for the way you raised me and all the things you exposed me to. Because you're a creature of habit, you just raised us the way you were raised. All I can do at this point is just pray every day that God gives me closure over what you did and the way you raised us."

I felt relieved. Her story made me understand that she was just a duplicate of everything she had been exposed to, and it allowed me to turn that corner of forgiveness that I had been struggling with my whole life.

That conversation furthered my journey of wanting to break off all those bad habits that I was exposed to growing up. I wanted to become the individual that God ultimately wanted me to be.

As a master of your environment, you have to take responsibility for the type of life you choose to live, and recognize the types of people and dysfunction you've brought into your life, if you have. Once you do that, it becomes easier to imagine your life without it, and you begin to realize how much it's been holding you back. Once you accept that you are just as much a part of the problem as the other person, it empowers you to actively start to find a solution. If not, the longer you let negativity stick around, the more comfortable it becomes in your life. It *becomes* your life. Your choices, decisions, and actions are affected by it. I want to tell you that the dysfunction doesn't have to be your life. You can break the cycle. All you have to do is decide *today* that you want better for your life and it will happen.

Being a reflection of your environment doesn't mean that you will *always* be a duplicate of your childhood. A lot of people are total opposites of their childhood environments. Some people grew up in a home that was so peaceful, so pleasant, structured, and strict that they are *desperate* for dysfunction, and they're on a mission to be the *opposite* of their childhood. Some kids grew up so sheltered that they work hard to act "regular" and end up rebelling from their nurturing upbringing. The key is to ask yourself *why* you need to have negativity in your life.

We've heard many stories of children who grew up wealthy, or stars who grew up with all the money they could ever imagine and completely sabotaged their entire life, with drugs, partying, and being rebellious. Anyone who didn't grow up with that type of money and lifestyle would wonder why anyone who was raised with so much wealth would be so crazy and wild. But it's just a pattern that most of these people aren't aware of. They're on a mission to try and find their own identity and they're rebelling against the family blessings that they were born into. Whether rich, poor, or extremely wealthy, every child during their adolescence is trying to figure out their own identity. I've heard on numerous occasions from people who grew up with money that they told their mothers and fathers not to give them anything, that they wanted to do it on their own. I guess that's their way of saying they want to find their own identity and feel a sense of fulfillment from achieving something themselves.

Imagine being a guy by the name of James Smith, whose

father is Mr. Smith the billionaire. Wherever James Smith goes, everybody talks about his father. His father had made his money before his son was even born, so it doesn't matter what the son does or how he does it, he's always on a mission to get out from under his father's shadow. Some people can grow up and be completely fine living like this, but other people can get rebellious. Some children may decide that they are tired of having everybody remind them of who their father is, as if they aren't worth anything, as if they are not even human because they haven't achieved nearly as much as their father did. This can make someone decide to take their life to a whole other level and be completely dysfunctional, as if they want to peel off the very identity that they were born with because they feel like they don't have one of their own. There is a flip side to every coin when it comes to breaking the cycle.

There's no way to tell how our experiences will shape us. There are always different perspectives and opinions on the same situations; it's the beauty of being a witness. If four people witness a horrific car accident, all four people will be impacted and react differently. It doesn't matter how somebody else is feeling about what took place, it just boils down to the way *you* were affected by it.

I don't want to associate dysfunction with anything positive, because it's not positive, but it can be educational: In order for you to recognize it and know what to stay away from, you sometimes need to go through it. In order for us to grow, we first have to be made aware of what our habits are. If I'm describing you, you should sit still, be honest with yourself, and try to put your finger on these habits and make a commitment to put these habits to rest one at a time.

If you are aware that there is too much unhealthy negativity in your life or relationship, you have a choice. You *must* come clean with yourself that you're *horrible* at picking friends, boyfriends, or girlfriends. If you are able to see and come to terms with the reality that you make bad choices about the people you invite into your life, then you have started to educate yourself and have taken the first steps toward picking better people.

The problems come when someone shows you their dysfunctional qualities and you keep them in your life even after you decided to stay away from these types of people. If you do, you're not making use of the knowledge and experience that you have. A lot of times we get into a relationship with a new person who is the exact duplicate of the person we just left. You may want to believe that because you left one dysfunctional person that things will be different, but you just jumped into a *new* relationship with the *same* person in a *different* body. Because you are still dysfunctional, you went from one to the next to the next. You left James and went to evil-ass Tony, or you left Kelly and went to crazy-ass Monica. All of these people are the same. If you are getting with the same type of person in different physical bodies, you're not growing. You have to grow, you must get away from them, you have to evolve. I, Tyrese, could say that I was in a relationship with four different people who were the same. Whatever negative characteristics they didn't have that would have reminded me of the girlfriend I had before, I figured out a way to bring that out in them. I figured out a way to bring more dysfunction out of them. But I finally saw the pattern and started to reprogram myself. I made a decision that I wanted better for myself and I was going to correct those habits and *control* them. I can say I am no longer that guy at all.

The people around you are a direct reflection of how you feel about yourself. I am not telling you to go out and break up with your partner right away, but if you're in a relationship with someone you know is not good for you, you have to question how much you love yourself.

I don't know if it's possible to eliminate dysfunctional tendencies completely, but what we can do is consciously stay away from dysfunction, or recognize it before it explodes, put things in perspective, and try our best to not let anything get out of hand. Think of dysfunction as the third partner in any relationship you have, who sits patiently in the corner of the room waiting to be invited into a peaceful situation so it can come in and do its job. Once you do this, you are another step closer to putting yourself in control of your environment. Control the negativity rather than letting it control you.

How Dangerous Is the Dysfunction?

Women and men will usually make a decision to move forward based on how their relationship seems. It may *look* safe but then someone gets hurt—emotionally, spiritually, and sometimes physically. People aren't stupid—we're just clueless. We're in the dark and we're uninformed about what's really going on and we don't know how to respond or deal with something we think we can't control.

Everyone's going to argue, so the question becomes, *How* do you argue? What are you saying while you're arguing? How far are you going to prove your point or to get your argument across? What are you using to drive your point home? Are you using secrets and very private personal matters as ammunition in your argument? And if you are, *why* are you bringing that up? People do this as a way to get back at the person they're fighting with when their mission is to hurt them—and that shows there's a lot more anger there than they are conscious of or want to admit to.

We can be upset about what someone did to us, but we don't know how to deal with it, and like a domino effect, this can create a dangerous chain of events. How do you know when your relationship will get violent?

Violence breeds violence. If you grew up in a house where you witnessed acts of abuse or violence, you may have learned to deal with problems by fighting, reacting, and getting physical. A lot of guys end up in jail because of what they were exposed to, and over the past several years there has been a growing number of women going to prison because they responded to, or initiated, domestic violence. These women got fed up with their husbands' and boyfriends' lying and cheating, or mental, spiritual, and physical abuse. Some discovered a new pain they could never have seen coming and didn't know how to deal with: that the fathers of their children were down-low brothers, living a secret homosexual life. Ladies, I really want you to hear me out on this: You may be going through or have been through something mentally, spiritually, emotionally, and physically traumatic, and you're running to your mama, friends, and neighbors to help you process and try to get through it. The worst thing you can do is *not* seek help. I have noticed that some women have too much pride and ego and associate getting help with being weak. But you must seek help, in the form of therapy and counseling, because what you've been through is some heavy shit. You can talk to the people you're close with all day, every day, but more than likely they are not going to have the answers. They can help you sustain your emotions but it doesn't mean they will dig deep and help you get the closure you deserve.

No matter the cause, today's women are reacting with stabbing or shooting. It seems like they are dealing with their emotions differently than they were twenty years ago, even if they had no prior criminal record or anything violent in their past that would predict their behavior. One of my close friends believes that many American women today have a more masculine energy and have lost some of their femininity because they've been through so much. I'm not sure if this is the reason, or if it's because widespread news coverage of such crimes ends up planting the seeds for another woman to commit the same type of violent act. No matter the cause, it only takes *one* second to mess somebody up bad. One second. How long does it take to pull a trigger? It's murder, and it's done in a second or two—you killed somebody.

It's arrogant for you to believe the next second belongs to you. It would be humble of you to make use of your next second in the greatest possible way you can. It only takes one second for your life to end, especially if you keep going back to situations that are abusive and messed-up. You can't assume that you're not going to die. Why go and sign yourself up for something that you know is not good for you? It only takes one second for an angry guy or girl to snap and hit somebody. It only takes one second for that man or woman to hurt you or kill you. When you know you're in a dysfunctional situation you've got to get out of there. It's arrogant to believe they will change. When someone shows you who they really are, believe it. There are a lot of people who have been on the end of physical violence or even death because they didn't pay attention to the clear signs of abuse in a relationship and convinced themselves that their partner would change.

In my opinion, the reason some men get physical toward women is because they cannot stop them from being disrespectful or saying evil things. I am *not* excusing this or saying it's okay, but at the end of the day, a man is usually physically bigger than a woman and can easily harm a woman with his bare hands. Many women are comfortable with being disrespectful to their men. A guy can ask his girlfriend over and over to stop saying mean or condescending things to him and if she doesn't listen he can get angry enough for things to get physical—especially if that's what he experienced in his childhood. He may think that the only way to get her to stop is by inflicting pain, just like his mama whupped him when he didn't stop acting badly. He remembers that back when he was young his mother or father would discipline him, and the pain from the whupping made him stop acting or talking a certain way. Some of the worst days I can remember were when I was bad as hell and my mama would make me go in the backyard, grab switches off a tree, and peel all the leaves off so she could use it to whup my ass. Some men may feel the need to go to the next level to demand respect in a physical way, because it all goes back to your childhood. In no shape, form or fashion am I justifying physical abuse; it's completely unacceptable. Messed-up situations and personalities with a lot of tension brewing could make things explode and get crazy.

At the end of the day, when communication breaks down, it can get violent if nothing he's saying is getting through. Because of what he's seen in his childhood, he thinks it's normal for things to get physical. And the cycle continues.

Once a man hits a woman she will either leave or just think twice before she starts getting on him for something, because she'll remember what he did to her the last time. In that situation, she loses all control of her environment. The smart thing to do is to get out of a relationship, especially if it turns violent. Unfortunately, that doesn't happen easily, especially these days.

Too many people go from one dysfunctional relationship to the next until they recognize the pattern. Find someone who isn't confrontational, who represents the new you.

The Cycle Continues...

You have more power than you think you do. If you have kids, how they turn out will be based on how you raised them. If they're exposed to your fighting and negativity every day, they will think that is the normal way to love someone. Don't let their childhoods and futures be affected by your dysfunction. I am asking you to break the cycle like I did.

Think about what you are creating because we often can't deal with the monsters we create in people. Some parents do not recognize that what they do contributes to who their children become. They only start responding when they see the outcome, when their children are grown, and even then some parents may not self-reflect.

Parents should look at what they are doing, how they are treating their children, what kind of environment their children are in, and what more they can do to create a better child. You have to think about when you want to stop hurting your children.

At what point do fathers and mothers reflect and realize how they influenced their child? In *most* cases, if your older children don't want to hang out with you or be around you, you have to wonder what you did. As children grow up and become a bit more mature, they may get rebellious and not want to listen to you. They won't want to hear anything you have to say, because they believe they're old enough to make their own decisions and do not want to include you. When they were growing up, how did you treat them? What kind of environment did you raise them in? What are your children witnessing now that will impact them in the future?

I can only imagine that a mother or father's worst nightmare would be to find out that their daughter decided to become a porn star or a stripper. It can be a shameful thing, especially if they went out of their way to raise their kids right, with morals, values, and integrity.

Even for some grown children the pain of dysfunction does not necessarily end. Some children believe that the only way for them to stop the cycle is to cut off that line so they cannot give their parents another opportunity to let them down or disappoint them. So whatever parents are doing that's messed-up, they are doing it at their own expense. Some children will not allow it to affect them.

A parent of an older child could say he or she did everything they could, everything they thought they were supposed to do, to try and be a great parent—and that may be true. Some children just ultimately decide to go off and be whatever they decide to be.

And so as a parent, you may be sitting back and thinking of everything you did, running down your list of all the things you did to show your kids love and wondering why you're not getting it back. I haven't experienced this with my own child and I hope that I never will, but I have witnessed this with other people and it can be a painful situation.

You are the master of your environment—and when your children are little, you are the master of their environments, as well. If you are all living in a cycle of dysfunction, look at how much you love yourself, set a new bottom line, and do whatever you can to break the cycle for them.

Parents who are dealing with rebellious teenagers or young adults should try not to own or internalize *every* one of your child's behaviors, or beat yourself up about what you did or didn't do that made them act in a certain way. Instead of shutting down, try to keep the lines of communication open to make your kids feel comfortable sharing their thoughts, so that they can work with you instead of against you. I have found that most parents and guardians would say their adolescents or young adults turned out better when communication between them and their kids stayed healthy and didn't break down.

It will be expected that kids will keep some secrets from you, but for the most part, parents I know would hope that their kids don't keep any substantial secrets. It may be hard not to react when your children tell you something you're not happy about. Some parents' approach can be very aggressive; as soon as kids tell the truth about something, some moms and dads are extra hard on them and may go on the attack, never letting them breathe and handing out extreme discipline. Your kids are either going to fear you and tell you the truth about everything, or they're going to fear you and never tell you shit. Every adolescent and young adult is trying to find their own identity. Either they're going to learn about life from you, or they're going to learn it from somebody else in the streets. Hopefully, they'll choose you.

Get in Control: Single Mothers and Fathers

You all deserve to live a life of love. You should always want to be an example for your children, and love is the best example you could ever give. I know this can be difficult depending on your personal situation, especially if you are a single mother or father.

Women—especially young, single women—can get overwhelmed when they get pregnant and are still very young themselves. A guy is either going to be there when the baby arrives or he's not. Some guys stay and some guys "escape" when they find out their girlfriend is pregnant. It's sad, but it happens all the time; it's an epidemic. Depending on whether the baby's father is around or not, a single mother may have a lot of anger and animosity toward the person who got them pregnant.

There is no excuse for any man or any *boy* who gets a woman pregnant to not try his hardest to be a father to his child. The thing is, if he was too young, he was never a man in the first place. You can't expect a boy to be a man. When one teenager gets another teenager pregnant, the guy becomes a father only as he gets older, but in those first seven, eight, or even ten years of the child's life, he may not be around. He may not be an active part of the child's life because he didn't become a man until ten years later. When he got his girlfriend pregnant he was just a boy, still into boy things, and nothing about being a boy connects him to being a father. He's still running around, clubbing, hanging out, freaking, wilding out. Meanwhile, the young woman who has a child is automatically forced to be more responsible because she's the one who is with the child.

When a teenage girl has a child she's lucky if her mother—who is now a grandmother—helps her raise the child. Her mother ends up raising her grandchild because her young daughter doesn't know anything about being a mother herself. Her mother didn't want her young daughter to have sex, but now she will try to get her daughter to finish her schooling and raise the baby. That's what happens if the young mother is really lucky. In many cases, young teenage girls who get pregnant have nowhere to turn. In a lot of cases, the young father is nowhere to be found.

An older single woman—in her twenties or thirties—may be more alone and without the help of her mother or other relatives. She may be feeling tired and frustrated about raising the child on her own, upset that she has no life and can't afford a babysitter. She is so consumed with taking care of the child, working, trying to figure out how she is going to support and raise her baby on her own, and she is desperate for the child's father to do his part. If a man doesn't want to step up and be a father, there is nothing she can say or do to get him to step up to the plate.

Unfortunately, there is such a thing as a man who has no interest in spending time with his kids. It pains me to say it, but it is true. There are two ways to react to this: The ineffective way is to feel guilty and depressed and let that negative energy take over and find its way to your child. The positive way is to focus on the only thing in that situation that you have control over: Yourself. Wasting your time and efforts on him will only make you tired, and cause endless frustration, because you will never get the results you want.

If a woman wants the father of her child to *act* like a father then she will have to talk him into it. When a father doesn't want to be involved, a woman will have to make him feel comfortable with being a father—something she may have expected him to be anyway. She may be wondering *why* she has to talk him into it and why he isn't there in the first place, but she will have to put that aside along with all the anger, hostility, resentment, disappointment, and bitterness she may feel toward him so he can feel more compelled to relieve her of the duties of raising a child.

The problem a lot of men have is that sometimes the most comfortable thing to do is not the right thing to do. A lot of us are lazy, and need to be taught that life is not about finding the easy way out. If you come at us too strong, we put our guard up, and do everything we can to protect ourselves.

I think it's cowardly for a man to not step up to the plate to be a father. However, if a guy is running away from his responsibilities, it may be because every time he shows up to do his part, the mother acts overly angry, hostile, and disrespectful; she may make the process of him picking up the child uncomfortable, messing up his day. He would rather stay away, leave her to raise the child on her own, and just send some child support when he can, because every time he goes to pick up his son or daughter, the child's mother makes his life hell, making it difficult to be a father. She may have told everyone she meets that he's not being a good father and—even if that is true—it will get back to him and bother him even more, which will cause him to not want to come around and help out. In this situation, the mother is allowing all her negative energy to overtake her. She is not acting like the master of her environment that she could be.

Women need to understand men and their responses and think before they act. There is no excuse for a man to not step up to the plate to be a father, but you should also take responsibility for your actions. You are the master of your environment and what your child is exposed to. You decide how you are going to react to the people who come into your home.

If you want the father of your child to be a *father*, you must get in control of all your emotions. Put aside everything you're mad about—and you may be angry about raising the child on your own, or that he's moved on to another relationship so quickly—and try to not get vindictive. You may want him to suffer the way you're suffering, you may want to say something to him to try and mess up his day, but the angrier you act, the more you will lose control and make the process of him trying to step up to be that father a living hell. It's natural for you to feel bitter and resentful that he's acting so irresponsibly and selfish (in the negative sense). However, taking all that out on him will probably discourage him from coming around even more. He may deserve it—and you may be angry that you have to ask him to do what he should have been doing from the beginning—but with that behavior you will only be undermining your goal and hurting yourself. You will be making him uncomfortable with coming over there and taking care of his responsibilities so that he won't want to see you for even the one minute it takes to pick up your child. As short and quick as it may be, getting his child can make him uncomfortable interacting with you and he could choose to avoid it for a long time.

You can make your feelings and opinions known to the man in question, but you have to create the reality you want for yourself and for your children. Remain in control of your emotions and do the responsible thing: Don't storm into his job, don't make a scene in front of everyone he knows, and don't scream and yell. When you go ghetto like that, you've lost control, and all you're doing is embarrassing yourself and making him more resentful of your actions. Contact him *privately*, in any way you want, and tell him that it is in his own best interests to spend time with his child. Push aside all your pride, hurt, jealousy, and anger and try to make him realize the error of his ways before it's too late. Inform him of his responsibility, and try to communicate openly and honestly about everything you expect from him in your relationship. Let him know that he is missing out on the greatest joy his life will ever know: his child.

The best thing you can do is be the mature one in the relationship. All you can do is be a grown-up and try your best to show him the correct path. If you still want him in your life for the sake of your kid, try to reduce the negativity you allow into your house. Inform him about all the wonderful things he is missing by not spending time with his child and do your best to help him improve and make better decisions for yourself and the kids, one small step at a time. If he is going to come around, it probably won't be a complete one-eighty-degree turnaround overnight. It's going to be gradual, and you are going to have to be patient with him. But if you want him in your child's life, then that is a small price to pay.

If he refuses to learn his lesson, then I encourage you to focus on what you can do to make your son's or daughter's life as rewarding and fulfilling as it possibly can be.

Don't allow the conflicts between you and the mother or father of your child to get in the way of your responsibility as a parent. When you coexist and create a child, your responsibility is to be a parent, period. Your child is affected by whatever you do. I am focused on being a responsible parent to Shayla, and her mother is, as well.

Kids are innocent. They have no control over who their parents are. Therefore, as parents, no matter how angry you may be at the mother or father of your child, you should not say anything negative about your child's other parent in front of your little one. Everybody loves to focus on the later stages of the relationship, when things got bad, but go back to the first stage, when you were first in love. At some point you decided to have a baby, whatever the circumstances may have been.

No matter how you feel about that man or woman, *you* had sex with that person on your own. That's what you decided to do. Take responsibility for that. Your child is innocent and has nothing to do with it, so you must not pump all the animosity and anger that you're feeling into the child's mind. You cannot try and turn this innocent child away from their father or mother.

I really resent parents who do that with their children because the child becomes confused and learns negativity too early in their young lives. I have seen this happen both ways and it is so painful for the child. You should try to not plant any negative seeds about your child's other parent, no matter what you're feeling.

I tell my daughter all the time, "Your mother is amazing. Mommy loves you, Daddy loves you," and I mean it. "I know Mommy loves you; she takes great care of you." While I'm with my daughter, I avoid having any conversations in general about her mother. I decided to make Shayla with my ex-wife, and I have no regrets about that. Even throughout the divorce and whatever difficulty we have had afterward trying to figure everything out, I still do not regret having a child with my ex-wife. I'm proud to be a father.

Conflicts *don't* have to be a bad thing. Accept their presence in your life as a blessing, that God is telling you that something has to change. Own every situation you find yourself in, because as the master of your environment, you are responsible for each and every one of them, good or bad.

Every person's relationship is different and all of our circumstances are different. Sometimes we give advice that can't be applied because it's for an individual situation, but in my telling my story, and sharing what I decided I wanted for me, hopefully someone will be inspired and make the effort to look at themselves and change.

The simple act of recognizing what influences our actions and thoughts is a huge step in understanding ourselves better, making more informed choices, and becoming the masters of our environment we know we can be. We can't change, adjust, or work on the things that we're unaware of. If we don't come to terms with the reality of where we are, what we're going through, and what is causing these problems, we won't change. We won't even know to change.

For a long time I blamed other people for a bunch of different things, and it boiled down to what *I* was doing to contribute to the situation. You can blame other people for how they are limiting you in some way, but you have to own it, you have to get clarity on how you are impacting the situation. Once you do, you have to do something about it. The first step to becoming the master of your environment and getting out of your own way is to *own up* to the part you are playing in affecting your life. Sure there are external factors, but there are ways to fix them. You can break the negative cycle.

Every aspect of your life should represent the things you speak as much as possible. I now take more responsibility for the responses I create in people, by being more conscious of my habits, the way I come off and the things I say or do. I don't want anyone to think that I haven't made mistakes, or won't make any more mistakes or bad choices. But you have to match your self-perception—how you see yourself—with reality.

When you become aware of what you're doing and how it's affecting other people and even, potentially, your career and your life, you must decide if you're going to change it or not. Success depends on your hard work and hustle.

As you make these changes in your life, remember that every lesson is a blessing. It's okay to hold up the mirror and look at your faults as long as each one of those lessons will help you grow and become a better master of your environment.

Chapter 4

Who Are Your Five People?

Just as your actions represent your thoughts, the people closest to you represent what you think of yourself. It's pretty simple. The people in your life—from your past and your present—make up your environment, and they can affect who you are and what you become.

As I've explained in the previous chapters, you are a direct reflection of your environment. How much you love yourself will affect how you carry yourself in your personal and business lives. If you don't love yourself, how are you going to know how to control your environment and the people in it so you can continue to get out of your own way?

All my life I made a conscious choice to surround myself with people who were better or reminded me of people who were better than those I grew up around. It was something I decided that I wanted for myself, even back then. I learned early on that *people* were essential to my growth. People like Angie, Gayle Atkins, and Reggie Andrews had given me permission to want better for myself.

Will Smith put this idea into words and made me look at it in a different way. During that same life-changing conversation, he told me something that really shook me up. He said, "You can often tell how far your life and career will go based on the five people you spend the most time with." When I first heard that, I paused, sat back in my chair, and started thinking about who was in my own circle of five—some were friends and others were business associates. I had to take a good long look at what was happening in my career and business relationships. I had to get past how long I'd known them, all the history we had, and ask myself, *Have we hit a wall? Do I really believe that my existing team can help me get to the next level?* I wanted to make sure I would get the kind of results and outcome I wanted and felt I deserved. I realized that I couldn't achieve the level that I was trying to get to in my career with the people I had in my immediate circle at that time. I ended up firing managers, agents, and lawyers and cutting off a lot of friends and associates. If I didn't think people could help me, I got rid of them. I still love them, we're still friends and stay in touch, I just don't work with them anymore.

Ultimately, you should be on a mission for a circle of five that represents your new train of thought and thinking. To simplify it, it's like if we all grew up as Christians, and you decide to start practicing Islam. We can obviously remain friends, but your walk and my walk are just a little different now because you're practicing a different religion. It's not that we can't hang out, but when it comes to religious talk and beliefs and our personal preferences, we're not on the same path anymore.

Right now, every person in my life—and I thank God that I'm able to say this—is in my life because I want them to be. There is nobody in my business or personal lives that I don't want. I don't hang out with people I don't want to be with. If I do, it's more for work, which is helping me along the way—that's networking, that's hustling, and you've got to do that to further your business. But for the most part there is nobody in my life that I don't want to be there, because I'm very clear about who and what I want in my life. To be in this space is the greatest blessing because it's such a level of clarity that I didn't have before.

Are You Being Celebrated or Tolerated?

I now live my life by the phrase *Iron sharpens iron*. Will had explained the importance of a strong circle of five with those words. I did some research and discovered they are part of a quote from Proverbs, chapter 27 verse 17: "As iron sharpens iron, so one man sharpens another." In other words, we need a strong circle of five because we need other people around us to make us better. Will told me that the reason I wasn't getting as far as I wanted in life was because I was trying to do it by myself. Once you have a few of the basic things figured out you won't necessarily need people around you all day, every day. If you get sharpened up, you're going to have great taste in people every place you go, so you can duplicate your circle and find great new people wherever you are. But when you're still trying to figure stuff out you have to submerge yourself in being around positive people because they will help make you sharp.

Imagine if during a fight, Muhammad Ali never went to the corner or let his team help him when the bell rang. That's what I had been doing. I had been boxing for twelve rounds without letting my team sharpen me up.

I had to figure out why I was settling for certain outcomes—the level of business execution, bad manners from friends, and other crap. If you've got people in your life who are keeping it real with you but whose advice is falling on deaf ears, then they have no value in your life—or at least they didn't in mine. Sometimes you have people in your life who are keeping it real with you but you're just not hearing them—like if your mom gets on you constantly, telling you not to do things. Unfortunately, a mother's nagging voice will usually fall on deaf ears when it comes to certain things because it's the voice you've been listening to your whole life, so you're just not hearing it anymore. But if somebody else's mother were to give you the same advice, you would probably listen because it's a *new* voice. So advice from Will Smith—the biggest movie star in the world and one of the most influential African-American actors in the game, a man who has been able to cross over practically every racial and discrimination barrier there is—was definitely going to hold a different kind of weight with me.

Is there someone in your life who is not contributing to your life or helping it move forward? Why do you keep allowing them in your life? Is it because you're lonely and you've only got so many friends, and if you cut off friends you'll be alone? If you're sad and miserable it's only because of *who* you have in your life. Happy people who want to enjoy life and embrace *all* of life don't hang out with miserable people. It's like oil and water—they don't mix. If you want to keep swimming in sadness, in misery, you're not going to hang out with people who enjoy life, because misery loves company, because *that's how you want to feel.* If you want to eat bad food every day like bacon cheeseburgers and all that, you're not going to hang out with a healthy person who eats salads or chicken. You won't mix the two, because your conversation isn't the same. If you're out of shape, it's because the people in your life are comfortable and will never say anything to you about it. Friends can tell you the truth or they can emphasize your addictions. If you want to change your life, you've got to change the people in your life. So you have to ask yourself, *What do I want for my life?*

You shouldn't hang out with anybody who you don't think deserves to be in your life. You may be running around complaining about your friends, but those are the people you *decided* to deal with. You may be complaining about your boyfriend or your girlfriend or a friend or the father of your child, but those people are who you decided to have in your life. In your mind at that time you had an idea about what you wanted for your life, and that's what you signed up for. So you must stop playing the victim and blaming other people because *you* invited those people into your life. Anything that ends up happening after you decided what you wanted is what *you* signed up for.

Think about the day you met that person you've been complaining about. Go back to that day in your mind and think about this: It doesn't matter how charming or how nice-looking they were. Think about how many people tried to talk to you that day, or even tried to talk to you that week, and you brushed them all off. You were thinking, *No, I don't like you. No, I don't want you. No, I don't wanna talk to you, I don't wanna give you my number.* You chose to ignore all these other people that week, that month, that hour, that day, but there was something about this man, or that woman, that made you decide this is what you wanted for your life. I'm sure you have a lot of reasons to go along with all the drama, all the problems and issues in your relationship. Well, some people need to hear the truth: You have horrible taste in picking friends! You have horrible taste in picking boyfriends or girlfriends! With all the people trying to hang out with you, roll with you, and inspire you,

you're ignoring good people and single-handedly picking the *worst* person in the room. What does that say about how much you love yourself?

You have more control of your hour, your day, your week, and your year than you think you do. Sometimes we need permission to take control of our lives. So let me tell you now: Stop dealing with your negative friends. If you want a better life, you have to change your environment and that includes those friends who are doing nothing for you. Stop hanging with that man or woman who is putting you down.

Decide today that you want to be celebrated, not just tolerated. What does that mean? To me, I've been in so many personal and professional situations where I've damn near devalued myself hoping to prove my value. In the beginning of my career my own insecurities made me act a certain way— being extra loud, cracking jokes, always wanting to be the center of attention—because I was fighting for acceptance, doing and saying too much to get people to notice me so that I may have even turned some people off. There are those who can be way over the top trying to win people over, jumping through hoops for their bosses or potential friends, but it doesn't take long for someone to decide how they feel about you. When it comes to relationships, one of the oldest rules in the book is: *When you run, I chase, when you chase, I run.* If someone is blowing up your phone and you get irritated, as soon as they decide to quit and let you be, all of a sudden you start chasing them. Now I've realized that if someone has already made it clear to you that they're not going to deal with you, you should find it in yourself to be okay with it and move on. Fighting for acceptance could literally drive you crazy. As long as you know your value and what you stand for, if one person doesn't see it, eventually somebody else will.

The truth is, your actions speak volumes—more than any words you could ever say. Even if you can talk a person into something, that doesn't mean you can live up to all the things that you convinced them of.

How much do you really love yourself if you still have people in your life you know aren't good for you? The people you surround yourself with—those you call, e-mail, and hang out with on your lunch break—are a direct reflection of what you think of yourself. If the people in your life don't have your best interests at heart, then you need to think about whether you're being celebrated or tolerated. You've got to switch up your circle so the people in it can contribute to your positive spirit and survival.

Emotional Access

I used to feel really bad about not hanging with some of my boys, the guys I grew up with. Even though we had a history, there were several times when I experienced someone saying one thing to my face and another thing behind my back, or found that people did things to put me in a state of jeopardy. I felt guilty about having more, about being the only guy in my whole crew with a car and money. Some of that was my own issue but there was some tense jealous and negative energy coming my way. But right now, at this point, it doesn't matter if I grew up with you or not, if you're not adding to my life, then you're taking away from it. There is no in-between, there is no gray area. It's not *Well, you add to my life sometimes and take away from my life sometimes.* No. It should *always* be about moving your life forward, progressing not regressing. Now, the people that I heavily associate with every day, whether on a business or personal level, add to my life.

At this point, I'm very clear about whom I give emotional access to, because when you interact with people you are giving them access to your emotions and mind-set and they can decide whether to mess up your day or not. Someone with access to you and your spirit can purposely cause you to become angry, disappointed, or uncomfortable or they can make an effort to be positive and uplifting.

There may not be an actual word to define this character-istic, but I believe there are some people that *get off* on trying to mess up your day. It does something for them to know that they can call you and say something or do something that will dampen your spirits. You know the kind of person I'm talking about. Your goal should be to try and get these people away from your circle as fast as possible.

Think about how your friends affect you on a daily basis. You could wake up in the best of moods and all of a sudden you get one phone call that completely messes up your day. This happens when you give wrong people access to your emotions. If you notice that there's a pattern with a particular friend so it seems like every time they call you or send a text message it always involves drama, dysfunction, bullshit, issues, and rumors, then you must decide to slowly but surely back away from this person because they're just consumed by negativity. Every time you answer the phone and actually sit there entertaining all their *stuff*, you're telling this person who keeps calling you with all their drama that it's okay to keep calling you—and that you're interested in what they're saying or support their calling you with the dysfunction. If you're listening silently, then they're not getting the message. But if you say to them, *Please don't call me with this stuff, man*, you will be discouraging them from calling you with all their negativity and at some point they will stop.

The old-school way of keeping it real is to tell them to stop calling you because they are killing your spirit with all their stupid issues. If you ask and they don't stop, there are some other solutions for getting away from these negative people. You could stop answering the phone when you see their number pop up, but that might not get them to stop calling you. I suggest you change your number, change your e-mail address, change your screen name. If you really think about it, how many people do you really talk to every day? If it's not that many, call those people you talk to regularly and give them your new information. Tell them to not give anyone your new information unless they call you to ask if it's okay to do it. This way, none of those negative people will be able to track you down. More than likely at some point, somebody may slip up and give away your new number to someone you're avoiding, but that will at least give you three or four months of them not calling with all the stuff that was driving you nuts and making your spirit negative. You will feel a real sense of peace.

Every situation is different and every friendship and relationship will affect you in a different way. Sometimes your friends may be going through a rough patch or a trying time. These friends are not out to intentionally mess up your day. During those times you should be there for them and have their back, and do or say something inspirational to help them go through it.

You have to be careful and guard your heart. You may meet so many people who seem like angels, but they're not—they're just trying to find a way to get in and chop you down, so don't let everybody in. Guard your heart and love yourself. You have to create walls and barriers, and realize there are certain people you have to block out, people you're only going to see once a month, especially if your relationship isn't healthy. Like I've said before, a lot of people talk about being selfish as a negative thing, but remember that it starts with *self*.

Your circle of five is a part of whom you allow into your environment. You're trying to get out of your own way and sharpen yourself up—this is being selfish in a positive way. As you work toward becoming the master of your environment, take better care of yourself and be aware of how people affect your spirit.

Making Changes

When I had to make changes in my business life it required a whole other kind of thinking—it was like a game of chess. You have to figure out the right time to make the change, you have to look at the history of each individual relationship and how it's going to affect how people perceive you and how you feel about yourself—the outcome of the way the world sees you and what is best for your life and business. A lot more goes into those decisions. When you do something that's going to cause a reaction, you must do it strategically. Don't do anything irrationally or without thinking. You should try and plan out your every move. A great first step is knowing how much you love yourself, and working on improving your positive energy.

It wasn't easy for me to make these decisions, so I went to church, which is usually what I do to get clarity and confirmation. I was thinking about firing a few people in my life whom I had been doing business with for a long time and who were, at that moment, technically in my circle of five. I got to church, and Bishop Ulmer, my pastor, just happened to be preaching a sermon that related to my questions. I cried and cried, because he was dropping it so heavy and giving me more details about how to go about getting rid of the negative people in my life. Ultimately, he made me feel more comfortable with the decisions I knew I had to make.

My pastor said something that helps me with all matters. He told us that if we're wearing a pair of faded jeans, we shouldn't try and patch them up with silk, because it won't match. This was kind of a perfect metaphor for what I was going through. In order to fix the hole in my life I couldn't patch it up with something that didn't make sense for my life, because it wouldn't fit and would fall apart eventually anyway. The people in my circle of five were not giving me what I needed. You have to figure out what fits for you—what you want and need in your life, to get to that better place. What reason could you have for holding on to someone who you know isn't the right match for you? Most people will decide to stay in something that they shouldn't be in because they don't want to start over. The process of getting to know somebody is very draining, grueling, and intrusive. Most people's biggest fear is that once they remove someone from their circle, that person will take their anger and spread all their business, all those deep dark secrets they learned over the years. At the end of the day, if you wake up every morning and that same bothered, miserable, or frustrated feeling is there, it's probably because you decided that you don't love yourself enough to walk through that door. When it's broke, it's broke. Sometimes love and relationships are like a broken glass. If you decide to touch it, it can cut your hand and cause you a lot of pain. When it's broken and you see that it's broken, don't touch it, just let it go. Grab your dustpan, sweep up all the pieces, put them in the trash, and move on.

So how much do you love yourself? How much are you willing to tolerate? You have to know whom you can trust. Figure out whom to trust by looking at who a person becomes when you turn your back. Trust should not be defined by who someone is when they're with you—it should be defined by who they are when they *leave* you. If they are the same person to your back that they are to your face, then they are people you can trust. Trust means staying consistent. I've got friends in my life whom you couldn't get to say anything negative about me, whether you're in their face or not. I've also got "friends" who have spread some negative and horrific lies about me when I'm not around but who put on all this positive energy when they see me. So you really have to look at the people in your life and figure out whom you trust.

You're going to have to make some serious decisions. Start by setting a bottom line. It's about timing, and everything requires a strategy. I had to think about the consequences. If I don't cut these people off, will everything I enjoy about my life go away? I had to ask myself if I was willing to say to my daughter, *Baby, the reason we're broke and I can't afford to send you to college is because Daddy decided to stay with people who weren't good for him.* Or, *I know you want that toy but I can't give it to you, because I stayed with these managers who didn't help my business.* What do *you* want for yourself? If you cut these people off— family members and so-called friends that you know are talking shit about you—I promise you will feel like I do today.

When I was thinking of what concerned me about people I had been doing business with for a long time, another bottom line for me was: If I cut them off, will they be on a mission to try and sabotage me? Will they run around and tell all my private and personal business? Those are the insecurities and concerns that anybody in the entertainment business has, but it can also pertain to people who work in other fields.

Sometimes, due to these concerns, we end up keeping some

people around we're doing business with, even though we know they're not good for us, because they know all of our secrets and it's just easier—it seems safer. I had to make an adult decision and find out what my bottom line was when it came to these relationships. The bottom line was, if I cut them off they're not going to kill me. That became a foundation of my being more comfortable with making these changes. I knew it by looking at their personalities and our history together. If I cut them off, they were literally not going to threaten my life or anybody in my family. I wouldn't be concerned about anything else they could say or do or try to do to attack my character or public persona.

I am now in a different space. I am so comfortable in my own skin. You can and should make these changes at your own pace, especially if you are uncomfortable with cutting off friends, loved ones, a boyfriend, or girlfriend. I always question how much I love myself if I want to keep certain people in my life. For me, I know there's only one Tyrese, and if I allow people to take me down to the point where I end up dying mentally, emotionally, or spiritually, I need to remember to love myself enough to tell them to get out of my life. Someone who talks shit about you today may do it again in one year or in two years, so you might as well cut them off now. If someone you're doing business with is not the best thing for you, then maybe it's time to remove that person from your circle.

A Season or a Reason: Necessary *vs.* Disposable Relationships

The problem with making changes is that a lot of times the people in your life are familiar—they're comfortable to you. They know you and you know them. I didn't want to not have a familiar face or energy around me, but as you grow up and mature you start realizing that some people are in your life for a season, and other people are in your life for a reason. The season with some of these people had passed but the people who were in my life for a reason were still there, and it made sense for me to go on this new path and this new journey and keep them in my circle.

People are either adding to your life or taking away from your life. There is no in between, and people who are not good for your life are disposable. Even if you grew up with friends and know how important loyalty and not forgetting your roots are, you will find that someone from your childhood can be in your life for a season or a reason. There are people whose thinking or approach to business doesn't represent the new you or the way you want to go about re-creating your life, so therefore they're disposable. You need to seek out and connect with other great like-minded people.

When you're making changes and deciding that you're going to do something, you're not always going to be joined by your friends, family, or loved ones. Some of these people will even try to discourage you from being whom you want to be or from doing the things you used to love to do because they're not as interested in those things as you are. When you set your mind on making changes in your life, that feeling of being alone—that feeling of not having support or love—could discourage you. When I was making my own transition, like when I was working on getting back into shape, it was really hard to get some people in my life to be on board with me. At some point they joined me but I was so fired up about it at first, I was so full-steam ahead, that they were probably shocked because it kind of happened out of the blue. Soon after that I started to see more clearly who my five people were.

When you decide to take that step and go in a more positive direction there are only so many friends in your life who are going to be able to handle or even wrap their heads around the new you. When these friends can't understand or support you, or they're just not within your thinking space, you don't need to stop dealing with them. However, you have to distance yourself from the people who aren't on your playing field, as far as the plans and ideas that you came up with for your life are concerned.

You may find yourself trying to get them to accept your plans for your life. If for whatever reason they decide to not approve or support what you intend to do and if your plans aren't firm and solidly etched in your mind, there's a strong possibility that they may talk you out of your goals, plans, and dreams. I've learned to shut up and stop telling people about all my plans because I don't want to get discouraged, and regardless of whether you end up succeeding or not, most people aren't happy for you in the first place.

If someone decides to not support you or have your back it's not always connected to jealousy; sometimes people just don't want to see you any differently from the way they already see you. Originally, your relationship worked because you were both broke; I call this being broke in harmony. You got along so well because you were in the same situation. Neither of you had anything going for you. So if you're going to step outside of the box, there's going to be a shift in the dynamics of some of your relationships. I will never forget when I did my first tour on the road, I came back and most of the people I had known forever weren't the same. Even if I tried to get them to look at me the same way, they just didn't. It took me years to come to terms with that. At a certain point, after fighting over and over to prove to people I hadn't changed, I had to sit still and say, you know what? I *have* changed! I've changed for the *better*. There's nothing about me—my thinking, my surroundings, the things I've been exposed to, the people I've met and things I've been able to do, my spirit, personality, confidence, knowledge of self, and my spirituality—nothing is the same as it was before. I have grown. Everything has changed, so therefore *I have changed*. Most people are in their own way and when you decide to get out of your own way they're still stuck, so they may not support you. It took me a long time to realize I could let some of the people from my past go.

Family is a much more delicate topic because these are people who will be around for the rest of your life. Most of us have people in our family we don't really get along with, whom we don't think very highly of, and vice versa. My suggestion is to limit the time you're around these people, and see them only when you have to. Keep your dealings with them under your control and within your comfort zone. Stop letting people enter your life against your will. Then, when you do have to see them, you will be mentally and spiritually prepared because you will already know what the outcome is going to be. Don't do these people a favor by hanging out with them, because your effort is best spent on those relationships that are a necessary part of self-love. We'll always have to deal with family members who do not have good intentions toward us, but we have the *choice* of when to deal with them.

There are certain people in your life who are necessary and can help you achieve your desired outcome, like your boss. If you don't get along with your boss, he or she is still necessary, so you have to deal with that relationship in a mature way. You have to recognize your role and your boss's role. If you don't like your boss or the way he or she talks to you or treats you, you can't let him or her get in the way of whatever mission you're on. If your boss makes your life miserable, think about coming up with a plan. Stay on the job for six more months to see if things change, save enough money, and around the third month, start lining up job interviews to try and transition from working there to somewhere else.

And then you have those people who are necessary, the people who do share the same thoughts and intentions as you. On the business side, you may say that you still want to clean house and just start all over. Remember that there are some people who are in your life who are still necessary to your success business-wise, because as you transition, these people have the thinking capacity and the spiritual capacity to transition *with* you.

In business, we will all have to deal with interesting and sometimes difficult personalities. There's no way to get around this. We have to endure these relationships for the sake of our future because they are necessary for us to get to where we want to be in life. When it gets hard, remind yourself that it's all connected to self-love. It may not seem like it, and it may sound like I'm contradicting myself by telling you to keep negative people in your life. I keep some high-stress relationships going because I care about my future and my daughter's future. I love myself enough to battle through. It's all about perspective.

I try not to surround myself with negative energy, or negative people. I have very few bottom lines but one of them is simple: I put out so much good energy, I take care of the people in my life, and if they don't mean right by me, I allow them to get rid of themselves. In other words, once someone has shown me their incompetence, once they've exposed that I can't trust them, once they have shown me who they are, then I'm going to recognize that they don't belong in my life and then I get rid of them. I'm *not* saying they can stay in my life and mess up my life as long as they want, until they decide to get rid of themselves. I allow people to show me who they really are. I don't want any negative energy bringing me down, or it will start a negative cycle that I can't afford.

If I can't trust them or find out they're sharing or telling my business, I say *Thank you!* It's a real blessing when people show me who they are early in a relationship because that's one less person I have to deal with. *Thank you for showing me who you really are, because you painted a totally different picture when we first met and first started doing business or started dating. I first was hanging out with your* representative, *but now that I've gotten to know you, I see your true colors, so thank you for allowing this to happen early on.* They dug themselves into a hole and they have to lie in it.

Those are my exact thoughts and feelings, but to take it to a more spiritual level, I've noticed in the last few years that God has stepped in and seen to it that things that don't belong in my life are revealed to me so I can get rid of them. For example, a while ago I was about to do a major business deal with someone and then decided to attend an event where I randomly met that person's friend. He started sharing several details about his friend that I didn't know, activities that I never would have wanted to involve myself with. I looked at the conversation as a sign from God, because I knew the odds were slim that so much information would be conveyed to me in such a random way. As I sit here writing this I don't even remember what led him to start mentioning this information. I let him ramble on about it and when our conversation ended, I thanked God over and over because I was a week away from signing a contract that would have made me partners with someone I now realized I didn't trust or know. My potential business partner had never revealed this information, and my own discernment, instincts, and intuition had never led me to associate this person with any sort of illegal activity. As much as I know about people and their energy, there are still individuals out there who know how to conceal who they are really well. But as I'm covered and protected by God, even when I can't see that something isn't good for me, God will eventually reveal it to me. I've learned not to question God when things are clearly laid out in front of me, so I immediately shut the partnership down and moved on.

When people dig a hole—if they lie, cheat, or do whatever they're doing behind my back—it's as if all I had to do was hand them a shovel. They say God is a forgiving God, and I know I'm supposed to forgive people for their mistakes, so I will help them get out of that hole just so they can walk away from me, because I don't want to bury anybody. I'm going to give them a shovel, and when the mistakes they made and the truth in who they are reveals itself, I'll make them aware that I knew what they were doing. If they're still digging and digging and the hole is getting deeper and deeper, they will end up falling into that hole. I'm going to reach out to help them get out of it, but once they're done I will be sending them on their way, because there's no second part to the hole. I only allow this to happen once.

This may sound harsh, but I'll never forget one time somebody said to me, "When you can't stand somebody and you know they can't stand you, just make believe they died in your mind. Picture them in a coffin." As crazy as that may sound—of course I'm not literally wishing death on anybody—when someone dies in your mind, they can't possibly affect your everyday existence because they don't matter anymore, they don't exist. That may be a little extreme, but there are some people who may be able to identify with that. For example, if you get out of a horrible relationship, it's going to make your life hell to keep thinking about the fact that your ex lives up the street, so it may help to get it into your mind that he or she doesn't exist anymore.

For a long time I was in the same broke, messed-up environment—gangs, drugs, killings, murders—but I decided to tap into the right people. We all know positive people, but the question is: Why don't we seek them out and include them in our lives? It's as if we're consciously making the decision to seek out *dysfunctional* people. Nobody talked us into doing that. Sometimes it's the result of peer pressure—people don't want to be seen doing anything positive because it doesn't seem cool, so we end up staying in dysfunctional situations because we're afraid to be the one turning our life around. An example of this is if you try to get some insight into your life and seek help from a professional, but your "friends" aren't supportive and try to make you feel stupid for going to get counseling and therapy to better yourself. They're refusing to even be associated with therapy because it's seen as a weakness. If they do this, they're trying to discourage you from growing or wanting better for yourself. How can someone you consider a real friend make you feel stupid or crazy for trying to get help because you're going through something that you cannot figure out? To me, it's crazier for someone to be crazy and not be willing to seek help for it. Don't let their negativity stand in your way. I can tell you that I wanted better for myself and was going to do it by any means necessary.

If you surround yourself with people who make you think you're not special, you need to get back to self-love. Find your own direction, be your own person, and don't be ashamed of who you are.

Don't think your life is going to end because you're not dealing with these friends anymore. Take the time to consider all of the relationships you have in your life, and decide for yourself whether each one is necessary or disposable. How much of your precious and valuable time is spent building relationships that don't help you get where you want or need to go? How much time and effort have you wasted on people who are trying to talk you out of your greatness?

I am not telling you to quit or give up on every one of your relationships. It's up to each and every one of us to decide for ourselves which friendships are worth saving. Weigh the pros and cons, decide if the positives outweigh the negatives and reconfigure your circle.

I found that having the right people in my life has made me happier. You have to create a happy environment for yourself, so that person you don't trust or like, who irritates you or annoys you, puts you down or stresses you out, has got to go. You have control of your environment. Situations will come up that you have no control over, but the people in your life can make a difference in your weathering the storm. You can't control when the storm gets here, but the right circle can help you get through it.

Chapter 5

Why Do Men (and Some Women) Cheat?

I want to take women on a little journey into the minds of most men. I'm going to keep it real with you, even though some of you aren't going to like what I have to say. Think of me as a big brother who has to keep it real with his little sister. I'm sure some of the guys reading this will get mad at me, because I'm exposing the things we sometimes do as men. I want you to understand why some men will cheat, how some men think, and our motivation when we decide to cheat on our girls. Let me help take the blindfolds off so you can stop playing clueless, and instead of freaking out and blaming yourself, you can keep your emotions intact. I hope that with the information I'm going to tell you, you can be prepared and make a controlled decision about your relationship.

There are a lot of different views and perspectives on what people consider cheating. One woman who was married for thirty years told me that sleeping with someone else is not cheating until you're married—but once you make a vow, it's a sin to cheat on your wife. Another woman said it didn't matter if she's married or not—if she's in a relationship and her man cheats on her, that's wrong and disrespectful and it hurts.

Is there a law of what cheating is? Everyone has a different perspective on it. Oscar-winning actress Mo'Nique shocked the world when she said that she doesn't want to cheat on her husband, but that he could have sex outside their marriage. Some women might explain that their husbands love sex all day, every day but they are not so sexually active—they don't want to have sex four or five times a day—so they let their husbands go out and do whatever they want. No two situations are the same.

A woman usually won't cheat on a man because she has much more self-control. It's not standard for a woman to cheat on her man, because most women have been programmed throughout their childhood to be a one-man woman. We're two different species; a woman's upbringing and the circumstances that informed her morals, standards, and integrity as a woman are much different than a man's. At the end of the day, it's expected that a man will cheat on a woman, but it's not expected that a woman will cheat on a man. Growing up, that's what I saw: Women wouldn't even cheat on the men that dogged them out. They would stay loyal and dedicated and determined to make it work.

A lot of us were programmed from conversations with our homeys throughout our childhood, adolescence, high school and college years that it's not just about the quality of women you get with—what she looks like or how hot she is—but the *quantity* of women you have sex with. That's what it boils down to—that's where guys get props. Meanwhile, women get scrutinized for having sex with a bunch of guys. They get called hos, tramps, hood rats. If they want to wild out, they pretty much can't because society chastises them. If a woman at college has sex with five or six different guys at the same school—even after a long period of time—and the word gets out, people will probably look at her as a ho and talk about her. But if a man has sex with five or six different women in one month on the same campus, he'll get all the props and love from everybody.

Marriage doesn't stop some guys from being curious about other women. My feeling is that you have to be honest about who you are and the way you feel and you have to put how you want the relationship to be on the table. It might hurt, but you have to allow a woman to make her own decision about how the relationship will proceed.

First Things First

Unfortunately, ladies, a lot of the ideals your mama instilled in you about what you need to do to keep a man are not necessarily true. If a man's going to cheat, there is nothing you can do about it. *If a man's gonna cheat, a man's gonna cheat.*

I'm not speaking for all men, but I'm speaking for a lot of guys I know. When a man cheats, there are usually no emotions attached to it. When a man decides to cheat he's just thinking in the moment: *That's a badass woman right there, she's sexy, she's giving me some energy, I'm ready to smash.* And just as easily as you can take off your shoes, that's how easy it is for him to go and make it happen. Most men don't operate from the space of morals and values or emotions. He'll just do his thing and keep it moving. It's sad and messed-up and unfortunate if he has a woman at home, but that's how easy it is. Does guilt set in? Yes. When a man gets home and looks his woman in the eyes and she's happy to see him when he's done dirty by her, the guilt can eat him up inside. But it never stops a guy from doing the shit again.

Usually women can't really understand that because for most women, having sex is so much more personal because a man is going inside of you—that's way more intimate and way more intrusive compared to a man, who can do it, pull up his pants, and go home.

Women shouldn't take personal offense if a man cheats, because it's not necessarily about them—it's most men's biology. A woman should not think that a man is doing all these things based on what she's not. I hope to create a safety net for women because I understand that they will drive themselves crazy trying to figure out what they did wrong and how to make a man stop cheating on them. Women will own the cheat, beat themselves up about it, and pick themselves apart, even though they couldn't have done anything to stop him.

I'm not speaking for *all* men, but the general consensus is that he's not thinking, *She doesn't cook well, so I'm going to see somebody else*, or *She's got a nice body but her hair is all wrong, so I'm going to see somebody else*. A guy usually doesn't *think* about that type of stuff. There are some people who do compare women but the general consensus is, if he's going to do it, he's going to do it. There are a lot of really perfect women out there who know they're perfect and whose men know they're perfect and they are still being cheated on. Even when you have a one-stop shop at home, if he's still going to go and get off, that's what he's going to decide to do.

Sometimes when a relationship doesn't work we become insecure, telling ourselves that being a good person didn't pay off in the end. I've heard several women say the same thing when they find out their man is cheating on them: *I cook, I clean, I wash his dirty drawers, I take care of the house and the kids, so why would he cheat on me?* Don't think any less of yourself because of what a man does on his own. It's not going to feel good when you find out, but it has *nothing* to do with what you're not doing or the fact that you could improve in any area. I want women to stop owning the fact that their man was cheating. Stop *owning* it, stop feeling like it's your fault or you could have done something any differently than what you were doing.

Men Cheat for Different Reasons

Cheating is fun for most, because getting away with that sneaky sex takes the sex to another level. I'll never forget the girl who confessed to me that she was a thief—and this was a pretty wealthy girl, too. She told me she used to steal anything; whenever she would go to somebody's house, she would go into the host's bathroom to find something she could steal. She said it got to a point where it became like a sickness, that it wasn't about what she was stealing. She didn't need any of the stuff she took—if she wanted, she could afford to buy whatever she was stealing. It was the *rush* of the steal that made her do it. Some people get that same rush from cheating. Sneaking around and getting away with it is exciting. It's a problem for men who are out cheating and doing whatever they're doing behind their girl's back and they can't stop themselves. Some guys get a rush from sneaking around and coming back home like nothing ever happened—it's like they have an alter ego and are living a double life.

Men have different motivations for playing the field. How far he'll go to maintain having all these beautiful women depends on whether he's used to dealing with women or not.

I know this will be hard for some of you to imagine, but anyone who knew me growing up will tell you that I was the ugly duckling who turned into a swan. People have this image in their head that I'm some sexy dude with the muscles and water dripping down him in the videos. But back then, my only way of getting attention was by being funny. I never pulled women when I was younger, or ever remotely heard the words "handsome," "sexy," "attractive." Once I got the Coke commercial and made my first video and all these girls started calling me sexy, it surprised all my friends and everybody who knew me growing up. They couldn't wrap their heads around the sexy image of me, and I couldn't either. When I started making some money and grew into my looks and was getting more attention from women, I was wilding out and doing my thing. It was almost like the other feeling I had after growing up broke, without a penny to my name: Once I started making money I was buying anything anywhere, as if I was trying to make up for all the years I couldn't buy anything. The same thing happens with the guy who didn't have any confidence or didn't hear he was attractive all his life. When he finally starts getting girls and growing into his sex appeal he may feel the need to get that out of his system and have some fun. That's what happened with me: I did my thing for years but calmed down as I got older. I'm now in a different space and more mature; I don't feel the need to wild out. Becoming a father definitely had something to do with it. I love women, but the aggressive urge to have sex with more and more women is not there as much as it used to be because I got a lot out of my system.

A cheater is a cheater, whether he's used to spending time with beautiful women or not. If he's going to go with another woman outside the girl he's in a committed relationship with, then that's just what he's going to do.

A man who is used to being with beautiful women is much more comfortable being around them and won't feel like he needs to *get* with every woman he meets. He is conditioned to it and treats everyone the same and doesn't tolerate the stupid shit. If he's one of those guys with a little money, career, good looks, swag, and the gift of the gab, if he's more of a Romeo, he's not trying to set women up to let them down and disappoint them, he's just kind of doing his thing, and keeping it moving. A man may have confidence, a swagger, and energy about him that attracts beautiful women, so it becomes a lifestyle that he's conditioned to.

For men who are used to dealing with beautiful women it's not only about the external. He may still deal with a bunch of different women who are all sexy and beautiful and attractive but it's not about proving it to himself or to others.

A man who is used to being around beautiful women is going to see things clearly for what they are. If you think of it as though a beautiful woman is a celebrity and men are her fans, it's not a realistic relationship. If a guy isn't used to hanging with these "celebrities," then to him a beautiful woman can do no wrong. She can say or do whatever she wants because he doesn't want to piss her off and make her run away; he is afraid of losing this sexy woman because he didn't believe he could get her in the first place. Like a groupie, he is starstruck and caught up in the idea of who he's with, how beautiful or sexy she is—her "fame." But when a guy is used to dealing with or being around "stars," he comes to see them as normal. He's able to keep it real and tell them the truth about their attitude.

Some guys have no confidence. These guys will either cheat to try and prove to themselves or their friends that they can get more women, or they will stick like glue to the woman they have because they're afraid they will never be able to get another woman.

There are a lot of men in relationships with beautiful women they can't stand, but they don't even realize that they're with that woman just for her pretty face. He may not think he can get another woman who looks like her, so he's going to hold on to this woman for dear life. He loves the feeling of walking into a room and having his boys and all his people reacting to how sexy and fine his girlfriend is and the fact that he was able to pull her off. He can't stand her, they don't have anything in common, they don't have great chemistry, but she's so sexy that she can torment him; she can torture him because he's not going anywhere. These are the superficial, external things that a lot of guys are not even conscious of.

A man who is not used to dealing with women may go and cheat on you—and may try to make that other woman feel as special as he's making you feel, because he feels like he needs to cling to as many women as possible. He may get greedy and over the top, making promises and telling lies and scheduling cheats. He will try to hold on to every little piece of something he can get ahold of and make every one of them think they're number one.

I don't respect a man who is in a relationship and hanging out with five or six different women, trying to make each of them feel like they're his number one and none of them knows about the others. I don't respect that—never have, never will. If he's ultimately going to cheat, he should get it over with and move on. He shouldn't follow up with texts and e-mails, stringing several women along emotionally.

Some guys feel like they need to get a lot out of their system, so they may run around trying to get with as many women as possible, even if that means cheating on their girlfriends. Men *and* women should try to have it all before they get married. When a guy is young and single he should do what he feels he has to do and go get it out of his system. A woman should want to marry somebody who's lived, who's been out there, because it kind of lowers the chance of his going nuts and feeling like he missed out on everything later on. Is this the ultimate answer to stopping a man from cheating on you after he gets married? No—it's not the be-all and end-all, and there is still no guarantee that he'll be focused. But it will at least calm him down a lot, and if he's not running around chasing girls, the chances of his cheating are slim to none.

For all the ladies that are reading this, I don't want to paint the picture that there are no good men left and that every man in the world needs to have sex with multiple women in order for them to never cheat on you after they get married. There are a lot of great men out there who are not into extracurricular sexual activity with multiple women. I want to let you know that those types of guys are out there.

Affection and Attention

I had a conversation with a guy who told me he was married for more than fifteen years. He was completely faithful and never cheated on his wife. He told me he used to wish he was her computer because she spent so much time working, consumed with everything she had going on, that he was completely ignored. He was suffering and it drove him nuts to the point where he had to get out of there.

This guy didn't cheat on his wife, but he's not with her anymore, either. The point is, his wife never had sex with him. He would talk to her about it but nothing ever changed. In this particular situation, the wife wore the pants in the relationship. As he was more subservient, she pretty much knew that the last thing he would ever do is cheat on her, so she just took complete advantage of him. She basically kept her sex hostage, and held back sex to prove her point. When a woman doesn't have any fear that her man will go out and cheat on her, I have to wonder how much advantage she will take of him emotionally. Most men in this guy's situation probably would have sought out another woman. If you're open and honest in your relationships—which I hope you are—then you have to really hear and respond to what your partner is telling you. A little affection and attention go a long way.

I've heard married men say that they don't know if they would have stayed married if it weren't for their mistress on the side. One of the most common testimonies from some married men that I've had conversations with is, *I am so married and I love my wife and I never want to* not *be married, but if it weren't for this other woman on the side, I would have divorced my wife a long time ago, because I'm getting something from her that I'm not getting from my wife.* One guy confessed to me that he doesn't just have his mistress for sex; she also provides additional emotional support. Because after a certain point, with his words falling on his wife's deaf ears, that other woman is helping him stay married. He explained that the other woman in his life *allows* him to tolerate his wife so much more, and that messed me up! He had been with this other woman for about ten years, so she was like his second wife. He told me that he loves his wife, the woman he is married to, but there is no way he would ever get rid of his mistress because he has an escape and an outlet. When he is stressed and miserable at home he goes to see his mistress and has a good time so when he gets home he doesn't give a shit about what he and his wife are going through. This wasn't a purely sexual relationship on his part; it was more psychological and emotional for him and I could see it in his eyes. Although this guy was open and honest with me about this other woman he has, I have to say that I don't respect having a woman on the side for years, a woman who is basically a second wife.

When guys cheat randomly it is usually not from an emotional impulse, but it does become more emotional if he's married and has a long-term relationship with his mistress.

I think a woman's biggest disappointment at the end of the day is seeing the woman her man slept with. If they see her and she's nothing special, it takes the pain to another level. What it boils down to is this: Sometimes if a man is cheating on you it's just about sex, it's not mental or emotional. It's not really about how much sexier this side piece is compared to you. It could boil down to her capabilities, the sexual habits, or freaky behavior that you may not have. And so she may not look like the sexiest woman in the world, but her skills are on a whole other level compared to yours.

Some guys decide to cheat because of what the other woman has. As crazy as this may sound, some guys in the hood want girls with the "good" hair, so they may cheat on their girlfriends just to be with these other girls. Some guys may decide to have a child with a woman just because she has good hair or a nice body and he wants to lock her down, to keep her in his life forever.

No matter what, don't own the cheat. Don't try to degrade yourself or pick yourself apart or internalize or own a man's choices. Don't compare yourself to the other woman, because you're never going to understand why he did it in the first place. And if she looks like nothing, you're really not going to understand why he was willing to leave you and cheat on you. You'll drive yourself crazy. There is no need to try and understand it all, you just have to be grateful that you found out about it when you did so you won't be in the dark any longer.

Anyone who goes through this—who discovers their man was cheating—is going to be distraught and have a meltdown. But when people show you who they really are, you have to believe it. If you're in a relationship with someone who should have won an Oscar a long time ago because you didn't get one inkling or feeling that there was anybody else in the picture, then that's going to hurt, it's going to hit you like a ton of bricks. But when you finish crying, get on your knees and pray and thank God that you found out about the situation when you did.

Be a realist and get out of the emotional space. This is the reality of today's man. A man's responsibility is to paint a picture and really make you believe that you're the only one. Our job is to make you feel secure in the relationship that you have. Unfortunately, he may be doing that with you and other people at the same time. If you are aware of this, then emotionally you can operate within that reality, instead of having it smack you in the face later, making you distraught.

Monogamous Men Do Exist!

Then there are the ideal husbands who have never cheated on their wives in their lives, and they've never wanted to, never attempted to, and never tried to, even though they've had ample opportunity. Unfortunately for our generation, we're programmed by the images we see in magazines and on television. Cheating seems so normal, and yet while many men cheat, some men are monogamous. Men who stick with one woman—whether he's married to her, engaged to her, or just in a long-term relationship with her—do exist. It's sad to say that these guys are pretty hard to find these days. Today, sex is so heavily advertised and prevalent in the media, with reports about cheating celebrities and marriages breaking up, that it seems like marriage is not a big deal, that it's easy to get married and get divorced soon after.

There are great men out there with integrity and the spirit of marriage, who live up to the God-given commandments. My mentor and friend Rev. Run told me that he has never cheated on his wife; he explained to me that he would never want to answer to Jesus for cheating on his wife, so for him, it's not even worth it. His commitment to God and his relationship with Jesus stops him from even thinking about it—and of course, he doesn't want to let his wife down. It all depends on where you're at and your perspective on life.

Men have many different reasons for *not* cheating. One of my friends told me that he doesn't cheat because he is deathly afraid of catching AIDS. One of his good friends died of the disease, so there is no way he could allow himself to be a loose cannon, even when he is surrounded by women who want to sleep with him.

I'll never forget chopping it up with this one musician I hired to play on an album. He had just finished touring throughout Brazil and I was telling him about the fun I had out there. I said to him, "Man, I know you got loose when you were in Brazil." And with a straight face, looking at me directly in my eyes, with so much conviction he said, "No, I just got my wife." It was as if I had offended him because I had assumed that he was like other men who were married and would at least occasionally do stuff with other women. Now, this surprised me, because it's unusual for me to hear a guy say that he's just got his wife. It's so uncommon to hear a married man talk about being with just one woman that it threw me that this guy was not even *remotely* entertaining the idea of cheating. Because when men start shucking and jivin' and talking that type of talk, even married men tend to chime in and talk about what they're doing and who they're messing with. Then he said, "You know what's interesting, Tyrese? You know what I love the most? I love that I still *like* her. I love that I still like my wife." This guy just *crushed* me because he represents the rare breed of man who's married and actually sticks to the commitments through the word of God, through thick and thin, till death do us part.

There are plenty of men who don't cheat on the women they're with and they're very comfortable with not cheating. They are out there for sure, and women should know that they exist.

My Number One Rule

As much as you would like to try to control a man, if he decides to do something behind your back, you really can't control him.

But this is my Number One Rule: A woman should make her man feel comfortable with telling her the truth about any and all things he has going on in his life. This will be the best for your relationship as far as being honest goes and it should be implemented with every aspect of what you're trying to get from your man when it comes to honesty.

When a woman suspects her man of cheating, withholding information, or having secrets about family or business matters, STDs, or past relationships—your first mission as a woman in your man's life should be to make him feel comfortable with telling you the truth and trying your best to keep your emotions intact. Women seem to be the victim of not getting the truth more often than men—that's just my general feeling. Unfortunately, even if you listen to my guidance on this matter and make them feel comfortable telling you the truth, some guys are not going to tell you the truth regardless.

The right responses and reactions will create a comfort zone for someone to tell you the truth. When a woman suspects something and comes at her man screaming and getting all emotional and loud, she's already breaking down, so why would he be honest with her? If she's already distraught and making it clear that her world just came crumbling down, a man won't feel comfortable telling his woman the truth. He's going to feel more comfortable with lying.

He wants to keep you happy, and keeping you happy sometimes means *not* telling you the truth. I said something similar in the movie *Baby Boy*: "I'm out in these streets every day telling these hos the truth. I lie to *you* because I care about your feelings." That's real talk!

So when your man comes clean with you, don't be insecure, don't be evil, don't get messed-up, because if you make him feel uncomfortable after he tells you the truth and you decide to stay with him, you better believe there's a strong chance he's not going to tell you the truth ever again because of the way you responded. For most men, telling the truth is the easy part. It's your *response* that can discourage a man from wanting to tell you the truth. Most men would say that women want the truth but they really can't handle it because of the way most women respond to a man telling her about whatever may be going on in his life.

Your guy could be out on the streets telling another woman the truth about what's going on with him because that other woman is making him feel *comfortable* telling the truth. That other woman knows what's going on—she may have a man, too. Make your man feel comfortable with telling you the truth so you will have the facts and be more empowered and in control.

Take note: Men also have to make women feel comfortable with telling them the truth. There are plenty of controlling and insecure guys who want to hear the truth and then flip out when they hear it.

Being more honest became my goal after I got out of my

marriage. I made a commitment that I was not going to hurt another woman if I could avoid it—I was going to make an effort to keep negativity and dysfunction away from my relationships.

When I was fresh out of my marriage and started dating different women, I decided to be completely honest and put it all on the table. I told the women I was dating that I was alone and not ready to settle down again. I let them know if I was seeing another woman at the same time and that at any point if she decided she was not cool with not being the only one and wanted to move on, I'd respect it. I allowed both women to make a decision whether to stay in the relationship or not. By telling them where they stood in my life I was giving them control and allowing them to commit to taking on any and every thing that comes with being with me. If they wanted to walk away they could, and I respected that.

Ultimately, I was out of a marriage and wasn't in the spirit of wanting to settle down or get right back into a serious relationship—I was alone, wanted some company, wanted someone to talk to, and it happened to be that I was enjoying the energy of two different women. Out of respect for them, I wanted to give them the heads-up that I was seeing other people so that they could decide on their own if they wanted to keep hanging out with me. I'm not justifying it and I'm not saying it's okay, but what I am saying is, I know how to treat a woman with respect. A woman will have to decide if she wants to go out with a man who is not being honest or up-front about their relationship, or be with a man who tells her the truth, so that nothing catches her off guard, and she'll be treated with the utmost respect while they're together. Ultimately, neither one of those women wanted to share me—they wanted me all to themselves—but they had to decide, *If I leave Tyrese, am I gonna be sharing a man with other women and not know about it, or be with a man who is more up-front about it?* Things didn't work out with one of the ladies but we're still good friends to this day and she told me that she would always respect me for being so honest with her.

I'm trying to help the women I'm with be more empowered by telling them where I'm at. Be honest and put all your shit on the table. Don't rob a woman of the opportunity to decide what she wants to do. When she's in the dark, she's not allowed to make a decision. She's not in control of her environment if she doesn't know all the facts.

Guys should try their best to be honest about what they're doing. It sounds a little unrealistic—most guys would probably say *Why the hell would I tell my girl that I'm sleeping with other people when I know it's going to hurt her feelings? She won't trust me, she won't want to be with me.* But you have to be honest *if* you're trying to do what I'm trying to do at this point in my life, which is not contribute to another heartache and not try to hurt or disappoint another woman.

Before I finish, I already know what some of you women are thinking. You would never agree to be one of two women who are seeing the same man. But the truth is, most of you already *are*—the difference is, he doesn't have enough respect for you to tell you that you're one of two.

Most women who are dating "eligible bachelors" are more than likely going to be one of two or three. The difference is, those men won't make you aware of it. They will not allow a woman to make a decision about what she wants or doesn't want in her life. They will keep their girlfriends in the dark.

I have a great deal of respect for women with a high tolerance for bullshit, women who can put up with a lot and take a lot. When my ex-wife and I were in the early stages of our relationship, I was still dating other women. She told me it was all right, that I would grow out of it. She's from Europe, where sex is not as big of a deal as it is here in the U.S., but that was still a very realistic and mature response. It didn't mean that she loved herself any less—and it didn't mean I respected her any less.

Respect has no rules. Every person's definition of disrespect is different. When a guy in a relationship has sex with another woman, it does not mean he doesn't respect his girlfriend. If his girlfriend is aware of what he's doing, then she has to be able to decide whether she is cool with it or not. If she has a problem with it, then obviously she should make it really clear to her boyfriend. The day she decides to throw in the towel, she's done. Some women who find out their man is cheating complain about it, but they stay in the relationship, so their complaints have no ground. But if a woman has *no idea* her man is getting with another woman, she's not on solid ground, either—she's not the full master of her environment.

You can and should establish honesty at the beginning of the relationship. If you make him feel uncomfortable about telling you the truth, you're planting negative seeds early on that could predict the outcome of your relationship.

When I first met the last woman I dated, I looked her in the eyes, and said, "There's something really magical about you and

I hope that I'm able to discover all of these things. But I wanna tell you something. I'm a very honest man. Sometimes I tell the truth and it may make you uncomfortable, because I'm bold in my truth. And the day that you make me feel uncomfortable with telling you the truth will be the beginning of the end of us. I would rather build this relationship on the foundation of difficult truth than plant seeds of deceit and grow a tree of lies and disrespect. That tree will grow but it will die eventually."

Let me give you another example: A while ago I had a business lunch with a woman who has been with her man for a few years. She said to me, "If my boyfriend knew I was having lunch with you, he would have wanted to come here and sit on the other side of the room while we were having our meeting." I was surprised because this was a business meeting. Clearly, neither of them had planted the seeds in their relationship to build trust. She allowed herself to create the kind of relationship with a man where she couldn't tell him the truth about what she was doing because of the way he was going to react and respond. She allowed that type of suspicion in her relationship, and her boyfriend was playing it.

This woman was also preventing her career from growing because her man was so insecure and on top of her about everything and had his own trust issues. You have to get to a point in your relationship where no flirtatious remark, no gesture another man or woman makes toward your partner, will allow them to pull focus from you.

I told this woman that she was slackin' on her pimpin'. Now, I don't want the word "pimpin'" to be taken out of context—it's about growing your opportunities. There are very talented women out there who could have more opportunities, but they're at home because their men are insecure and have conquered them and made them feel discouraged about going out and being seen, networking, and socializing. Their man is threatened by the presence of other men, especially successful men. Men get threatened by emotional access and know how to say and do all the right shit. So these women don't grow their business. Opportunities don't come from your sitting at home—you've got to hustle! The lack of honesty in this woman's relationship was keeping her from controlling her environment.

I told her, "My approach to business is, out of sight, out of mind. If you don't get on people's radars and in their faces with your brand, image, or ideas, they will never consider things or people they don't know about." This woman had met her boyfriend while she was doing her thing, but he was talking her out of being who she wanted to be. If a woman allows that, men will succeed in conquering her. When a man is putting that much emphasis on what you're doing, he may be trying to overshadow what *he's* doing. He may be making her nervous about every move she makes just so she can stop paying attention to whatever *he's doing* on the side.

If you keep things aboveboard and honest, then there will be no room for any antics or suspicion. Plant the seeds of honesty in your relationship early on.

Women Are Much Better
Cheaters Than Men

A lot of the reasons why women cheat could be the same reasons why men cheat—they're looking for the attention or affection that they're not getting from the man they decided to be with. Generally for women, it's more emotional. Their man might not compliment them or touch them. He may not be nurturing or stimulating her mentally.

Some women think, *My husband is so busy, he's consumed with what he's doing, but I want some attention and something wild in my life*, so they schedule time when the other guy can get her right.

Many women are much better at cheating than men can ever be because their whole thing is premeditated, whereas for most men, our cheating happens in the moment. Some dudes need to leave cheating alone because of what I call the "Popcorn Rule." A lot of guys think they're being slick but they leave popcorn kernels down the hallway so it's easy for women to pick them up and eventually find the whole bag. One of my mentors told me that if you're not good at something leave it alone. Where there's smoke, there's fire, and today's women are really smart.

Women are more detailed. They come up with a real plan. They know how to clean up all their tracks. Sure, some women are sloppy and get caught, but it seems to me that for many women, cheating is premeditated—so well planned out that their man will never know. I had dinner one night with a girl who told me she's cheated on each of her last five boyfriends and none of them knew. She told me this comfortably and had no problem with it. A woman will know when her man is out of town and she will know when he's getting back in town. She knows his schedule, and she makes it all happen around that. It might be more dishonest than just a onetime thing, but I can't make any call on that.

Don't rob a man of the opportunity to move on or not because you're keeping him in the dark about what you need, what you're doing, and who you really are. And if you put it all on the table and tell your man what is lacking in the relationship, what you would like more of, all the things that you want, and he doesn't love you enough to make any adjustments, then you need to pack up your stuff and go. Because at this point you may decide to uncharacteristically start cheating or lying. When you're mad, frustrated, and miserable, you may act upon impulses and start doing things that you would have never remotely thought of doing before.

Positive Affirmation: Men Are Like Babies

Some women are going to know their men cheat. They're going to scream and hoot and holler because they don't want to make a guy feel comfortable about sleeping with another woman behind their back because it upsets them. This will slow a guy down a little bit but it won't stop him if it's something he wants to do.

Your reaction is important especially if you're in an abusive or dysfunctional relationship.

Even if a woman isn't cheating on her man, she could still be causing him the same amount of pain as when a man cheats on her. A woman can cause a man a lot of pain in the way she talks to him or if she overlooks his efforts. If the level of pain a woman feels when a man cheats on her is at a thousand, when someone's efforts are overlooked—if a woman does not recognize when her man steps up and does the things she asks him to do, applauding her boyfriend and making him feel good—she's causing the same amount of pain that a man can cause her by cheating. Most women will say there's no way I can compare these two kinds of pain, but they are the same. They're both pains of pride.

Women have to think of men as babies in that we need positive affirmation. When a child makes a mistake, you get on the little child, but as soon as they stop doing something wrong or correct it, you applaud them and encourage them and recognize that they did a good job. That's important for a child and it's also important for an adult. Men are like babies. We make mistakes and get chastised, but once we correct the mistake we want to be applauded, and we want to be reminded of the fact that we did something really good. We want a woman to make us feel good that we stepped up to the plate and delivered on whatever our women asked us to do. We don't want our efforts to be overlooked.

Many women don't understand that if a guy finally decides to hear his woman's cries to stop hanging out with certain people or stop doing something, he needs her to make him feel amazing, because he never would have stopped doing it if she hadn't asked him. You ask a guy to stop doing something because you love him and when he does, he needs to be applauded and appreciated for actually stepping up to the plate.

Many women just complain, scratch, bitch, and moan about what a man's not doing and what they want him to stop doing over and over and over, but once he stops doing it, they don't follow it up with an equal amount of appreciation. That affirmation is extremely important in a relationship—for both men and women. A woman has to recognize when her man steps up to the plate—like if a man is being an amazing father. If your man is not a horrible father to your child or messed-up like some of your girlfriends' men, he deserves to be applauded, loved, and upheld. It's expected that a woman will be a good mother, because women are naturally nurturing and embracing. If you have a man who is a great father, you have to make him feel amazing about being who he is and what he is when it's going great.

Maintain positivity in your relationship with positive affirmation because men have emotions, too. It could be for the smallest thing—setting the table, running the bath, picking up the kids. Just say thank you. Make him feel like you recognize and appreciate the things he's doing.

Of course, a man should also do this for his woman! Men should not overlook the work their wives or girlfriends do in the home. She may take care of the kids and the house full-time and may even be working on top of that, too. It takes a lot of patience and tolerance to be around a kid twelve hours a day by yourself. Women need positive affirmation, too. If somebody never gets affirmation or compliments, it's similar to getting put down. Women and men have to be recognized and applauded for the great people they are in their relationships and their lives.

I've learned that most women think that if they give their man too many compliments it's not a good thing because he will think he doesn't need to step up or go to the next level because his girl is happy. But there is no such thing as too many compliments. You can never assume that your significant other even knows that you think of something as beautiful or flattering or considerate until you speak on it. For example, I was in a relationship with a woman, and the smallest things would make her look at me and say *Wow*. She would wake up and find that I had plugged in her cell phone and laptop. She thought that was the biggest deal—and I had just thought she'd need her phone in the morning. Or I may notice that my girl is running low on gas so I'll fill up the tank when I'm out getting groceries. Small things are a big deal to most women. It's important for a man to do those things, but it's also important that a woman lets her man know how special it was to her because it will motivate and encourage him to keep doing those things for her.

The more positive affirmation you can give to your partner, the further the negative spirit will be from your relationship.

Are You Keeping Sex Sexy?

Rev Run told me that he did not have sex with his wife until they were married. I respect that, but I don't know if I could do it. Some people may say it's good to test the waters before you dive all the way in. For us Christian folks, the Bible tells us to not have sex before we get married. Do I respect that? Yes. Have I practiced that habit? No. Do I respect celibacy and people maintaining their virginity before they get married? I respect that one thousand percent and I encourage every man and woman out there who has not yet had sex to maintain their celibacy and save themselves for marriage. But I think the mind-set of most people today is that if they are already sexually active, and they are planning to marry someone who has not been sexually active or a person they have not yet slept with, they may be rolling the dice. They will wonder what they are signing up for. They may worry that they could be marrying bad sex. You may not want to find out that you have no sexual chemistry—or that you will have to work on taking your sexual chemistry to another level.

At the end of the day sex isn't everything but sex is very important in most relationships. Sexual chemistry can keep a lot of people in dysfunctional relationships or marriages. Two people may not get along, but when they get into bed and have sex it is incredible. They figure that if the sex is that magical there must be a way for them to figure out their problems. Then there are other relationships where people are on the same page in every way *except* their sexual chemistry.

Women out there who complain that they don't want a minute man should know that *no* man wants to be a minute man either. Any man in this world will want to get in bed and go at it for a nice, decent amount of time, but you should feel that it's a compliment when a man has an orgasm really fast—it means you've got some great sex. Have you ever looked at a porn and asked yourself why the guy is taking so long to have an orgasm? It's likely because the woman he's having sex with has had so much sex that while he's inside her he doesn't really feel anything. He could go on forever, and nothing will ever happen.

You have to know if your sex is worth a man deciding he has everything he ever imagined at home and has no need to get it from anywhere else. This may be hard to hear, but I want to keep it all the way real with you. Are you sexually capable of keeping your partner focused? Ultimately, if a man is going to cheat, he's going to cheat whether you give him the best sex or not. But you have to know if your abilities are up to par. Do you know how to go down on your man? Are you willing to get better, to know what pleases him? As long as you don't feel demeaned or uncomfortable, you should work on keeping each other happy at home sexually.

The same goes for men; it works on *both sides*. There are some women who can't depend on their men to make them happy sexually, so they go off and find another man or end up pleasing themselves at home with vibrators and other toys. A guy has to please his woman and figure out how to do it better if what he's doing is not working for her. Figure out a way to step up your sex game, get creative and change it up. Do what you have to do to keep it interesting and keep the sparks flying.

I encourage all of you to keep your relationships going. If you have any type of trouble, on any level, talk to your pastors. When you get married, the devil gets busy. If God is in it, it's right.

Allow your self-value and self-love to determine whatever your decision is going to be in a relationship. I cannot tell you that you need to leave your man if he's cheating, because every situation is different. My rules and my laws are mine. If a woman ever cheated on me, one time, the relationship would be over. I know that's a double standard, but I'm all about honesty at this stage in my life. It all depends on where you are within the respect you have for yourself. Allow the respect you either feel or don't feel to determine what you're going to do. Some men are worth keeping.

You have to figure out what your relationship is worth to you. Think about it according to the 80/20 rule, which I heard about from *Why Did I Get Married?*: When your relationship is 80 percent good you always wish you had more of that 20 percent—whatever it may constitute for you. So the question becomes, do you leave your 80 percent to go out and find someone who could offer you more of the 20 percent you're looking for, or do you hold on to your 80 percent and work hard at improving your relationship one percent at a time till you get to 100? When it comes to love, winners never quit and quitters never win. Most men are not able to say that our actions, approach, or outlook are the same that they were even two years ago. Men *can* change and it takes a firm, strong, and solid woman who has a very high tolerance for bullshit to introduce us to a better version of ourselves. Women should assume that men are just creatures of habit, and for most of us, our approach to love, relationships, and women is based on our upbringing. But there is a way to change all these things. You just have to be patient and not give up on us.

Chapter 6

Do I Love You More Than I Know You?

A lot of times we don't know we're in a relationship that we've set up to not work. Some of our relationships are not healthy from the start—and I'm a victim of it, too. You're in a relationship and you say "I love you" when you see him, you kiss, you hug, you're—*supposedly*—making love. But do you love him more than you know him? Do you love her more than you know her?

You would figure it's impossible to love someone as much as you do if you barely know them, but sometimes our emotions are too far up the street. Let's say when you first meet each other, you started on First Street. You're thinking, *He's sexy* or *She's got a nice body* or *He's tall, he's handsome*—all the things that attract you and can make you start to catch feelings instantly. Just a few weeks into the relationship, you barely know each other. For example, you only know each other up to Tenth Street, but your emotions and your feelings and your love are on 150th Street.

It is possible for you to love someone more than you know them because it's really hard to control your feelings. Your feelings can be based on a lot of different things. They can be based on physical attraction or sexual chemistry. A lot of the time, sex does it—you feel more connected to someone because you were intimate.

I've learned that someone being sexy as hell can speed up the feeling called love. I happen to be a fan of exotic-looking women with all-natural everything—flat stomachs, nice breasts, and big asses. Those things can do something for a man and can make a man decide instantly that they "love" you.

I've also heard women say that they loved a man really fast because they had a great conversation, he was physically attractive, and there was great sexual chemistry between the two of them. All these things are very impulsive but don't feel very impulsive while you're in it.

Other times, the reactions and approval you get when your homegirls meet your man, or when your homeboys meet your girl, can make you love somebody much faster than you know them. Some women are on a mission to prove all their homegirls wrong. For example, when a woman finds somebody really special—or someone they *think* is special—they run around bragging, showing off, telling everybody they know. That's when things go left because you run around painting this picture of this man you feel like you know and have all these feelings and thoughts for, and then the truth as to who he really is comes out. That's when you get embarrassed, when you start keeping secrets from your friends, because you painted the picture that the person you're in a relationship with is just *amazing*, flawless, and near perfect before you discovered that they're really not.

Some people will read this and say it *is* realistic to fall in love with somebody, make a commitment or marry early and get to know them on the other side of marriage. I am sure it *does* happen, but those are very unique, one-of-a-kind godsend scenarios. There are plenty of stories out there about love at first sight. It does exist. There are plenty of people that are able to say *I met my wife, I looked her in her eyes, and I knew at that moment that she would be the woman I marry* and they go on to get married and spend the rest of their life together. But what *normally* happens is that people create in their minds the picture of the perfect man or woman just to find out that they are not who they thought they were. For the most part, these impulses—*I gotta love you, I gotta settle in, I gotta be your wife, I gotta get serious and make everything happen*—these moves (like the ones we see on reality television) set most of us up for a major letdown. How do you try and get in front of *emotions, impulses,* and *love?*

When you love somebody more than you know them, you set yourself up to be disappointed when you discover the things about their personality that drive you nuts. If you love your man or woman so much, once their negative characteristics or the truth about who they are is revealed, the reason you're so hurt is *because* you created the idea in your mind as to who you thought they were. Based on who they *appear* to be, you're already in love. You're thinking, *I love him so much, how can he talk to me that way?* Or, *I love her so much, how can she treat me that way? How can she embarrass me like that? How can he front on me like that? Why is she putting me down and making me feel like this? Why is he cheating on me? Why is he looking at other women while he's with me? Why does he treat me differently when we're alone compared to when we're with his friends? Is he ashamed to love me publicly the way he does privately?* These are the thoughts and feelings that run through most people's minds. Would you really feel this way about somebody you claim to love so much?'

Stop acting like you know him or her—you *don't!* If you are able to control your emotions a little bit and take it one day at a time, you'll be able to stop yourself from going so far up the street and actually love him as much as you know him. Then, once you discover all of the things that you don't like about him or her, you'll save yourself from heartache.

Paint the Picture Along the Way

The problem with most of us is that we create an image in our *minds* as to who the person we're with is, and we think we have them all figured out, but we *don't*. We don't know who they are! You're projecting your feelings and your ideals on that person. When you create in *your* mind who this person is and the picture is already complete, you think you know who they are and what the outcome of the relationship will be. You are trying to predict the future. You've created this whole image in your mind based on your *fantasy*. It's not real—you set yourself up to be disappointed. You have to discover who this person is along the way.

My ex-wife and I had this thing we used to say: *You have a paintbrush in your hand, and I have a paintbrush in my hand, and we're going to paint the picture of who we are and what our relationship will be along the way.* We painted the good, the bad, and the ugly so that we wouldn't allow ourselves to be let down by a picture already completed in our minds. Our marriage and our relationship was going to be a work in progress.

Put the paintbrush in your hand and paint the picture along the way. Add the good and bad to the painting as you discover it so the love story you're building with this person is forever evolving.

In most cases you're meeting someone's representative. Everybody is presenting their best self. Like a magician, their mission is to use smoke and mirrors and make you believe the things you're seeing with your own eyes. While you're sitting in the audience watching the show, you're going to be convinced that 98 percent of the things you see with your own eyes is really happening. That's how it works with most relationships. You let down your guard and surrender your heart, spirit, and mind to this man or woman based on what he or she *appears* to be. In a lot of cases, they will live up to what they present themselves to be, but unfortunately many others won't. So once someone gets comfortable and they get relaxed and they fall into the everyday routine and you start to see their true colors, sometimes you won't like what you see.

Allow yourself to take the time to get to know somebody before you start loosely using the words "I love you." Ask yourself, *Do I* really *know this person I'm with, whom I'm telling I love? Do I really love this person, or is it a sexual thing, or is this person just an answer to my loneliness?* Are they filling in some void, that you had everything else but a man or woman in your life? Since you met this special person, you allowed your feelings and emotions to go five thousand miles up the street instead of *pacing* yourself and really taking the time to feel it out and give them time to show you who they are. Try your best to give yourself that time, so you will be in control.

I don't want to make anyone think I'm denouncing the way they really feel. I can't tell you that you don't love the person you're with. I just want you to consider that the reason you may be so hurt and disappointed and let down by these personality traits and habits and the way he talks to you or the way he acts or how she embarrasses you sometimes, is because you're so in love. Although it may be challenging, try your best to learn to love somebody *within* what you know about them, and don't allow your emotions to go too far up the street too soon. I've learned to try and get to know someone at the same pace as loving them. In that way, I can try and love things that I discover, that might have frustrated me later.

Be cautious and prepare your spirit for the things you don't know about this new person in your life. You're going to be so much more deeply wounded emotionally about their cheating on you or lying to you if you are in love with them than if you just *like* them.

You'll have contained your emotions as much as you possibly can so the things that you discover about their personality won't impact you so strongly. You're probably still going to be shocked, and whatever you discover will throw you for a loop, but you won't be distraught or depressed. You can be in a place where you try your best to make a non-emotional decision about the best way to deal with what you discovered.

Today's Sexual World

Sometimes a woman will feel like a guy acts differently toward her as soon as she sleeps with him. He's not calling or texting as much, or it seems like she isn't on his mind as much as she was before. From a man's perspective, there could be few reasons for this: Either he was only in it for sex, or the sex wasn't worth the wait.

He wanted to have sex with her as soon as he met her but she decided to filter him out and get more comfortable and acquainted with him. He was patient and understanding that she wanted to take her time but now that he's slept with her, he's done.

If sex is the one thing he's after, when he finally gets it, he will just think, "Mission accomplished." The smoke and mirrors he created—saying and doing all the right things to make her feel more comfortable about giving him what he wanted the whole time—disappear. When it finally happens, it's over and done. You may notice an abrupt change in the amount of attention that you're getting, because if he was only after sex he was probably willing to do, say, and be whatever he needed to in order to get it. You may feel used, taken advantage of, and dirty.

The other side of it is, Was the sex worth the wait, for either of you? A woman will normally wait to have sex—that's standard and I understand it. But in general most men are ready to go. I had a conversation with a woman who told me she made a guy she was dating wait five months before she slept with him and once she did, everything completely changed. He stopped calling, he stopped texting. When you make somebody wait that long and you're both so excited to finally be going there, with someone you've been wanting to go there with, and he ditches you afterward, you have to wonder what went wrong. Honestly, my first thought was that the sex she gave him probably wasn't good.

If he was waiting for three months or five months he probably cared about her, but it also means that while he was giving her some quality time—and because he was not celibate the way she was—he was probably getting some action on the side while his focus was on her.

This is the truth about the reality of today's sexual world and it has been going on long before we got here. There's a double standard: A woman is *supposed* to make a man wait, because the fact that she's not running around having sex with random guys says a lot about her self-love and self-preservation. There's a difference between men and women: If a woman is dating more than one guy, she's not necessarily having sex with everybody who takes her out. As soon as a woman meets somebody and decides that she likes him, she's not usually opening her legs and having sex with him right away. But a man is different—he is not going to ask for a woman's number, open up doors for her, or ask her to dinner unless he's trying to sleep with her.

Some men are aggressively about sex in relationships because they feel like they have to overcompensate for their lacking in the "man's man" department. He may want to have sex with a woman right away because he doesn't feel he'll be able to hold on to her for too long, because he's not mature enough to keep her mentally stimulated. Maybe he's not the intellectual type, or he's not a charmer or the Romeo who knows how to say all the right things. Or he might not have a great job, or be confident about certain aspects of his life. But he knows how to please a woman in the bedroom—that's the one place he's secure—so he thinks that if he gets her into bed, she'll at least be running around in a fantasy world with some little birdies chirping above her head.

There's a double-edged sword when it comes to deciding when to have sex with a man; you can't win on either side. If you give it up too fast and nothing comes of it, then you'll run around feeling like a tramp, and if you make a man wait, trying to get to know him, and he breaks up with you soon after you sleep with him, you'll still feel like shit.

If you make a man wait a long time to have sex with you, you have to ask yourself if your sex is good. What I'm saying could bother, confuse, and may even piss some women off, but I believe in keeping it real. You have to know whether you can please your man so he won't go out and try to be with any other woman sexually. The same can be said for a man. If a woman decides to cheat, it may be because her man wasn't pleasing her in some way, sexually or otherwise. These are some of the risks we take when we enter into a relationship. Clearly, if a guy ditches you soon after you have sex, then you didn't know the real him.

Unfortunately, I can't give women a time frame of when they should sleep with a new guy—that's different for each woman and each relationship. At the end of the day, if a man's mission is to have sex and that's all he's focused on, then a woman is technically not meeting who he really is. She's meeting the man who is saying and doing all the right things to get what he wants.

Getting Past the Physical

If you go through the filtering process of getting to know somebody, hopefully in the midst of their getting to know you, they will fall in love with the woman or man in you, outside of their initial sexual thoughts of you. This is the beauty of God's plan, and I hate to include God in this discussion about sex, but there is nothing like meeting a person whom you only intended to have sex with, and discovering the woman in her or the man in him. You discover their heart, their integrity, that they're loving and nurturing and they have a story and do not wear some of their horrific experiences on their spirit.

Something like this happened with my ex-wife and me: We ended up connecting after we starting talking and sharing our stories. To be honest, all I wanted was so have some fun, get loose, and be seen with a pretty, sexy girl, but I ended up discovering her personality. She had this discernment and intuition about her that was so powerful, and it was those things that made me fall in love with her. I discovered her layers, so it became more than just physical.

It's possible that a person's intention could be just to be seen with you and have sex with you, but they can discover the woman or man in you and your relationship can become so much more than just a rendezvous. So at the end of the day, just make sure you step up your qualities so you're more than just a one-night stand.

Don't be one of those people who are not about anything—

who have nothing interesting going on in their life, who are just going through the motions. People like that can't keep someone's attention when they're having a conversation. So read, study, tap into knowledge, and hang out with people you look up to and admire. Allow yourself to grow beyond what you are, and that way you won't just be seen as a physical, sexy being. Allow yourself to discover the layers within *yourself.*

Be comfortable with who you are, and that way, when you go and have a conversation with a person you're interested in, he or she can get past the sexual and physical and actually tap into and fall in love with the woman or man in you, not just the *external* you.

A woman has the power to get a man to see her differently than how he sees her at first. His initial intentions might be sexual, but because of her qualities and the content of her character, the things she stands for and her integrity, she can get him to look at her completely differently than the way he looked at her when he first met her. A woman has that control. A man has that control, too. A woman may think she's already into a guy physically, because of his body—because he *projected* that image—but as she gets to know his thoughts and the way he's thinking, her love for him can go to a whole other level.

Figure Out *You* First

Get comfortable with yourself and be confident in that. It's a harsh reality because men and women are unpredictable. At the end of the day, just take care of your sandbox and if you invite somebody to play, be prepared for them to mess it up. As long as you have your sandbox in order, you don't have to worry about anything else. Have your integrity, your spirituality, your morals, and the things you stand for all in order, so a person who comes into your life won't be able to dictate who you are. If you don't know who you are, then you're leaving yourself wide-open and vulnerable for someone to come in and define you. If you don't know who *you* are and you have no sense of direction, then you're going to believe whatever they're saying to you—even if they're saying horrible things about you.

A lot of men are great orators. They've got what I call the gift of the gab; they know how to talk you into doing all kinds of stuff. Because you *believe* you love your man so much, you can find yourself doing things, going places, dressing or acting a certain way that you would never in a million years have seen yourself doing before. You make all these adjustments based on *his* comfort zone and your being in love with him. This could be a good thing or a bad thing because no two relationships are the same.

Here's an extreme example of how a man can use his gift of the gab to influence a woman's mind and thoughts. I've never been in the same room with or witnessed a conversation pertaining to this, but a pimp is going to have a conversation with a few different women and he's going to be able to convince them to stand on a street corner, in rain, sleet, and freezing snow, to sell their bodies. These women will dress the way the pimp wants them to dress, and stand there on the corner for however long he wants them to, and they will bring all the money they're making from selling their bodies to him. Anybody with any kind of common sense would say that doesn't make sense, why would *any* woman be willing to do that? But it happens every day because of this thing called the gift of the gab, when a man is able to convince a woman to do anything he wants. All we can do is hope that you don't fall in love with someone who is able to manipulate your feelings and emotions and get you to start doing things or being a part of something you could never see yourself doing.

If you are so desperate to be loved and get affection and attention, you may be willing to do almost anything. The worst thing you can be is a woman or a man with no sense of self or direction, because if you don't know who you are or have no sense of direction, when you run into a man or a woman who wants to present *their* directions, you're going to do or say or be anything they want you to be.

The gift of the gab can be a good thing or a bad thing. A man or woman who uses this gift in the right way can literally change your life. They can make you aware of something and pass along information or help you get through trying times, and you can come out on the better side of a situation. I've been in relationships and have had a few female friends that were trying to figure things out, and I guided them through with my perspective and ideas. Because I don't have any malicious or vin-dictive intentions toward the women in my life, they trusted me, believed me, and rolled with my sense of direction, and for the most part they ended up thanking me and feeling great about decisions I helped them make. But not everybody is me. I know I've got the gift of the gab, and I'm a man with many layers—spiritual, mental, and emotional—that many women gravitate toward. If I had messed-up or malicious intentions toward them, I would be the worst-case scenario.

Here's another example: I'm a Christian. My feet and my heart are on solid ground with my relationship with Christ, even though I'm still getting to know Him by reading the Bible and furthering my dealings with Christ. But if I wasn't solid or firm in my religious beliefs, if I were feeling lost and in need of direction, anybody who is a part of a cult or other religious group could easily influence me to be a part of their group. When you don't have a sense of direction and someone presents their own ideas, you may immediately jump on board. Depend-ing on what you're into, that could end up being a good or bad thing. Ultimately, if you are insecure, if you don't have a sense of direction or don't love yourself enough, you could end up in a very dangerous, life-threatening position.

Figure yourself out and define yourself *for you* as much as you can before you get into a relationship. That way, no one will have any wiggle room to manipulate your emotions. If you don't know who you are and you don't know what you think of yourself, once your man tells you what *you* think of *you*, you're going to believe that, because it's coming from somebody you think you love, who you think loves you. So when you go out to random clubs and go places where all these guys are giving you all these compliments, you won't believe them, because that's not the way your husband or boyfriend feels about you. If your man calls you a tramp, you won't think you're beautiful or sexy or intelligent or sophisticated. That voice will constantly play in your mind, because it's coming from somebody whom you know and love.

It's not just a matter of knowing yourself, because you can know yourself but not know the person you're with. You have to communicate and welcome honesty. Put everything out there. Make your partner comfortable. My approach is this: You should feel like you can go to sports bars together, you can go to strip clubs together, do anything together, because you're *friends* and make each other feel comfortable about being who you are. You're not trying to make each other anything other than what you are and if you want to make him or her aware of what you're thinking about how they are acting or presenting themselves, then you can be honest and tell them. There is no need to hide anything, because you prepared each other with details about your life. With preparation and knowing each other's reality comes a different comfort zone about who you are.

Try and be more comfortable with who you are. Pimps say the way to break down a secure woman is to point out her flaws. Even a very confident woman will focus on her flaws once you make her aware of them. If you say one negative thing about her, she will brush it off, and come off thinking she's beautiful, but she will think about that forever. The natural instinct is to be defensive and come back at you about whatever comment you made but she will be thinking about it all day and all night.

Some beautiful women are attracted to thugs and run away

from dudes who tell them they're beautiful and fine all day. They want someone who will not be caught up in their looks. These women I'm describing are not *used* to thugs; they're used to guys who make them feel beautiful, but they end up going for the thugs because they want to be challenged.

Many women are so confused and they don't even know it. They say that they want Prince Charming: the considerate and respectable guy, the most attractive guy, a guy they can take home to their mama. But then when they get him, they get bored because they're trying to *conquer* the man and shape him into what they want him to be. They get him to stop doing all the things that irritate and annoy them and then they get tired of him, and want to go after a wilder party dude who will ignore them and treat them like crap and challenge them. Some women want to be the one who was able to slow that wild train down, to mold him, train him, and change him.

Every mother tells her daughter to find a man who will treat her like a queen and give her the best that life has to offer. She could be the first lady of somebody's life, but she doesn't feel challenged anymore. She'll get bored, so then she ends up looking for that thug who seems more "real" and treats her like crap. She doesn't really know what she wants and can end up in a relationship that has a lot of potential for danger.

Some women and men try to take on the role of Jesus Christ and "save" women, and women try to "save" men. They think, *He's wild, he's crazy, but that's all gonna change and I'm gonna work with him,* and their boyfriend becomes a pet project. You're taking on this load, this full-on responsibility to try and change the man and you complain the whole time you're going through hell, but it's something that *you* signed up for. You knew he was a thug when you started dating. Remember, life is a menu. Whoever and whatever *you* order is what will be delivered to your table.

In my opinion, most women who end up staying with a man they know is not good for them—disrespectful, condescending, evil guys—do so because these guys are *familiar.* They get in the spirit of believing everything he's said about her. She believes him and has taken on the character of all of the negative things that he said about her, and she carries that with her everywhere. He has broken her down little by little until she feels small. He has her so insecure and he's crushed her spirit to the point of no return so she's not going anywhere. She's going to stay right there, because he was on one mission—to break her down—and now that he's succeeded, she's not in control.

When someone tells you that they love you and in the same breath they say all of the evil shit in the world, *those* are the people you will most likely listen to. Those are the people who shame you and mold the way you feel about yourself.

We all have a little genius in us and we just have to take the time to discover it and nourish it and figure out exactly what we can offer the world. Most people are not on a mission to discover the genius within. They just want to duplicate and be like most of the things they see. Take the time to discover the genius in yourself. You *cannot* define yourself by your boyfriend or girlfriend.

You have to figure out the way *you* feel about *you.* Take that leap of faith, break the chain, and start surrounding yourself with people that elevate you. Does this sound easier said than done? Of course. It's not easy to walk away from anything if you've made yourself believe it's good for you or feels like love.

Telling and Hearing the Truth

Try your best to take your relationships slower. And more than anything—I can't stress this enough and I've said this before—make your boyfriend or girlfriend feel *comfortable* with telling you any and all things. Women and men mess up in the way we react to the truth. Some of the things this person drops on you can be a shock to hear if you've already developed serious feelings, and with our reactions we can discourage somebody from telling us even more about their lives. We can scare them away so they may think the stories they're sharing are turning us off. Be careful not to discourage somebody from telling you all the different things that you need to know about them, so that you can better decide how you feel about them and if they are the right person for you. Just hear them out and try to stay calm. Don't overreact, and if you do, don't overreact harshly. You're having a conversation with this person and you want them to open up because they are your *friend*.

I'll never forget one woman who told me the advice her mother gave her. She said when you have been in a dysfunctional and miserable relationship—if your ex ran you over emotionally, cheated on you, took advantage of you—you have to decide very selectively whom you will share that information with. As you're getting to know each other and you're giving your new boyfriend or girlfriend all the details about what your ex put you through, you're basically telling this new person in your life, who thinks the world of you, how much you tolerated in a previous relationship. He may think he can cheat on you and you will pretty much take it. By revealing what you put up with, you're giving this new man permission to do dirty by you. This person is thinking you're A-plus, but you could end up devaluing yourself based on all the things you tell them about your past.

I would love to tell you that you will know someone after three or six months, but that wouldn't be the truth. In some cases, a first impression can last a couple of years. It all depends on you and the level of comfort you create within the communication between you and your boyfriend or girlfriend. In some cases, a person could be a pathological liar—someone who is lying and more comfortable with lying regardless of how comfortable you make them feel. They just want to lie—but more than anything, they don't want to allow another person to know everything they're thinking or everything about their past. They're staying in their comfort zone and holding you at arm's length because of their insecurity that if the relationship doesn't work out, you will walk off knowing all their business. They do this for self-protection and self-preservation.

There are two sides of the coin. Of course, you want to build your relationship on the foundation of truth, planting positive and trusting seeds will grow into a great tree. However, in some instances, opening up and telling this new person you're seeing all the details about what you went through or certain things in the past could be used against you. I still suggest that you be open and honest but you must take it upon yourself to decide *how much* of the truth you want to reveal when you first meet them. It can be a progressive process, where you feel them out and gradually share the good, the bad, and the ugly.

Open up, tell the person you're with all the things that you're comfortable letting them know, but remember that you also have the power to create the mind-set of your new man or woman. You want to be the master of your environment. Sometimes, in order to stay in control, you have to limit what you share until you feel like you fully trust the new person in your life.

Powerful Women

Some men are intimidated by educated women with self-love and self-respect, so they go and get what I call "low self-esteemers"—people who don't have any goals, who don't want anything for their lives. They can talk a scantily clad low self-esteemer into believing they're nothing, but they can't do that to a woman who knows she's something and has a lot to offer the world.

Some women may wonder why they are alone if they're sexy, attractive, and successful. They make a lot of money, have a career, and can pay for dinner. Most likely it's because men see them as a threat. A lot of guys are intimidated by women who are educated, goal-oriented, and want more and better for themselves. In addition, a woman who makes more money than a man is a threat to a lot of guys.

As I said earlier, a successful music producer once told me he was dating a lot of women from overseas because he had noticed that a lot of successful and smart women in the U.S. have a very masculine energy and an overly aggressive mentality. For many of these women the money, the independence, and all the materialistic things become the power. They've got a career and all this success but they're still lonely. These women want a man but they have to know that straight from the gate they're a threat until they make themselves *not* a threat. They have to recognize that if they have the power they don't have to use it. A powerful woman should learn to not treat her man like an employee.

You should understand that there is something about the power and confidence and energy of a strong independent woman that can be very intimidating to a lot of guys. If a man is intimidated by who you are, you shouldn't be with him because it's going to be an ongoing struggle for you to try and make him feel more secure as a man. If you meet a man you're interested in, even if you have more than him financially, get to know him and allow him to try and fill that void in your life. If he wants to be all the things you don't have in your life, you should allow him to be the man he is.

Don't ever dumb yourself down or lessen yourself, but in order to make people feel comfortable, you have to make them feel like you want to know more about them. Create a better playing field: Elevate them and make them feel important, because you already know you're important. You don't have to tell all about your success right off the bat, even if you are used to getting someone's attention that way.

Are You Acting Out of Insecure Impulses?

I met a very successful woman who owned a company with dozens of employees. We had just met and she dropped so much information on me—how much she was making, how much her house cost, how big her house is—and I was sitting there the whole time listening to her, thinking, *That's a whole lot of information you're dropping on someone you just met!* I thought she was trying to impress me, but it also showed me that she was insecure. She wanted to impress me and get my attention, but she was also telling me that she thought she was nothing without all this *stuff.* It seemed she didn't think she was nearly as special as all the things that came with her. She didn't think she was impressing me herself, as a woman, so she felt the need to tell me about all the things she owned. I would love to believe that she was telling me all that because she was proud of her accomplishments, but it felt like it was coming from an insecure place. I'm sure you ladies out there are able to say you've met plenty of men who have acted the same way, giving you too much information about what they're worth, the cars they own, their jewelry, and other materialistic stuff. They just met you and volunteered all this information. I see this behavior as the result of insecure impulses. What they're saying is, *Even if you're not impressed with me I hope that you're impressed by all this stuff I have.* And the materialistic stuff says nothing about their character.

You don't have to tell everybody your business. Most people

are not aware that their bragging and talking about all the things they have shows that they are coming from an insecure place. You don't have to be desperate for a reaction, that feeling of being sweated. You don't have to run around dropping names to make you seem cooler.

Talking about the things you've accomplished is cool. You have to be proud of what you're doing, but it has to come from that space. If it seems to others like your material success *completes* your self-confidence and you show off to make sure the other person is impressed, you're probably not impressing anybody.

The more you brag about all the things that come with you, out of insecure impulses, the more you're setting yourself up to have a man or woman take advantage of all that. Don't allow the money and the materialistic things to define who you are.

The difference is in the mind-set and the thinking. You want to get to know someone—and vice versa—based on who you are, not what you *own*. Think of it this way: It doesn't make me a great man *because* I'm pulling up in a Maserati. There just so happens to be a great man *sitting* in that Maserati. A woman should be able to say *I love the man in the car.*

From my experience, I've found that if rappers, singers, and athletes take off all their jewelry and bling, they can seem like the most insecure people in the world. One night a few years ago I went to a club with a rapper. There were a ton of fly women all around us. He leaned over to me and said, "Man, these women are all going crazy—and I don't even have any jewelry on." Of course I knew that it didn't matter if he wore jewelry or not— the women were sweating him because they were fans. It was surprising for me to find that some of his strength and his confidence was connected to his jewelry.

A similar insecurity can be linked to women and their makeup. Some women believe that a man will flirt with them, trying to get their attention or a phone number, only when they're all dressed up and wearing makeup. For women, the idea of going out without their makeup on makes them uncomfortable, but men will still find them attractive. Most men like the natural look; some women have told me that they've had more guys try to talk to them when they put less attention into what they wear—like when they run to the supermarket in sweats and Ugg boots with no makeup and their hair barely done—compared to when they're all dressed up. It's not always about what you have or what you're wearing that can make a person interested in you.

A lot of people don't know when they're doing things out of insecure impulses. I was in a relationship for several years and every time I made a mistake I tried to fix it by buying things for my girlfriend. When she wasn't impressed with me because of something I did or the way I acted, I would take her on a crazy shopping spree and buy her *stuff* to get her to forget what I did.

I needed to buy her something and have her so consumed with what I was buying for her so she would decide to stay with me. Back then, I wasn't as mature or confident. I didn't know how to sit down and have a conversation and work things through. I thought that with all the *things* I bought I could keep her contained and happy. But it wasn't real—it was just smoke and mirrors.

Try your best to get to know the man who comes with all the stuff he comes with, and really figure out how you feel about him. If you're clearly hooking up with him because of *who* he is and everything that comes with him, then have a ball—but don't try to make it into anything else than what it is. Don't create a fantasy too soon in your relationship.

There was something about the foundation of love back in the day, the way love and marriage was instilled, so that marriages and relationships lasted. It seems like only the people who have been married for more than thirty years know how to fight for love or have the patience for love. Today, we don't seem to have the same integrity, patience, understanding, bond, or connection to live up to the vows. What were they doing back then? We know they were reading the same words in the Bible. They were exchanging the same vows, but how is it that they are still married decades later? With all the divorces and broken relationships, it seems like we're not working at it at all. I go back and forth sometimes, wondering if I was a coward for giving up on my own marriage, even though I know there was too much negativity in front of our daughter. What was it back then that made it possible for those long-married couples to actually stick to commitments? Did they know themselves better? Did they take the time to get to know each other and to love each other? That's something I always think about.

I also wonder why so many parents and adults talk and talk about wanting their kids to marry and settle down, but they don't advise us on *how* to maintain a successful marriage and get through all the trying times. So many couples will end up filing for divorce because their parents have not made them aware of how to make a marriage work—and maybe their own marriages didn't work. How do you make anything work if you don't have all the tools or information to make it work?

Sometimes when I think about my childhood I remember my parents and my friends' parents emphasizing two things. They told us, *When you grow up, be successful and go make a lot of money. When you grow up, find the one you love and get married and you'll live happily ever after.* Back then, it was a very exciting thought but as I got older I wondered, *After I make all of this money what do I do with it? After I get married, how do I stay married?* Most people anticipate getting engaged and it's a confidence booster and it's beautiful but have they really sat down and thought about all the ins and outs of marriage, or if they even have what it takes to be a husband or a wife?

Today's version of love is very different. If you have parents who were married for thirty, forty, or fifty years, they may have instilled in you what love is. But they fell in love back when the dynamics, challenges, and issues we have today didn't even exist. Some of you may disagree with that. An old man I know who was married for forty-seven years once said to me, *Tyrese, y'all ain't going through shit. Y'all ain't doing nothin' new when it comes to love. There have been the same challenges and obstacles that have been around for all these years.* I wasn't willing to argue with him, but I walked away and I had to disagree. I feel like sex on television, nudity in magazines, girls in music videos with their bodies out, all of these things weren't as prevalent or in-your-face. Things were more tactful. There was drama because parents were concerned with the images that were on television. Now, unfortunately, all of these graphic images are available.

I still believe in love. I know that true love exists in the world and I still believe in the morals of love, whether it's old-school or new-school. But there are many different challenges right now to making love work. Maybe if we get to know ourselves first, and try our best to get to know the one we're saying we love, we can achieve the love we're picturing in our minds.

Chapter 7

What Is Your Purpose?

I dream with my eyes open. I want to become what I see. When I was younger I was always looking around for something better—because anything had to be better than what I was exposed to. And I still do that. Sometimes we need to see things in order to discover what we want to become. I want you to be able to say *I see the invisible, I hear in silence, I climb invisible stairs, having faith in God with no points of reference.*

I wanted to become more like the people around me, like the mentors and pastors who impacted my life in a positive way. I saw what they were doing with my own eyes, and I was influenced by what I saw. We should all dream with our eyes open. Look around and see the positive things in other people's lives and actions and imagine better for yourself.

A lot of times the people around you are going to make you feel uncomfortable about what you're doing or where you're going in life, when you're trying to do something on the next level and special. You should always expect people to be negative and not get behind you, but *don't* pay attention to any of that. When people are discouraging, I like to say *Only those who can see the invisible can do the impossible.* What that means for me is that others might not see what *I* see for my life. People will try and discourage me or create the spirit of doubt in what I want to do with my life and the different directions that I want to go in, because they don't see what I see. I am seeing the invisible and I'm looking to do the impossible.

I was that kid who got laughed at because I was trying to sing. When other kids at my behavioral school hated on my singing, I didn't listen to it, because that's what they were *supposed* to do—badass kids were supposed to be down on everything new or different. Even some friends and family made comments and laughed at me, because I was the funny guy—but years later they were calling and asking for concert tickets. So at the end of the day, be comfortable with your *individuality*. So many people are going out of their way to fit in and be accepted by everybody. Forget that. Do your thing.

Get comfortable in your weird. The word "weird" from my understanding means quirky, different, being an outcast of some sort. People that are different see things differently; they don't really go about their life trying to be a part of the things that normal "cool" people would be a part of. I have a great deal of respect for people who are considered weirdos, especially *smart* weirdos. Weirdos have been forward-thinking revolutionaries, game changers, and world changers. People used to call me weird because of the way I think and my outlook and my approach on life, and I used to have a problem with it. But I finally said, if all these amazing things I've accomplished—all the blessings coming back to back, the success I've had in different areas of my life and career—if all this came from my being a weirdo, I'm going to wear my weird as a badge of honor.

I stayed positive and I stood my ground because I loved what I was doing. Nothing people said could take away my joy. And the thing is, a lot of my confidence comes from my knowing I've already heard my worst no—being a kid, standing in a parking lot, asking people for their shopping carts so I could make twenty-five cents to pay for the DASH bus to get to school, and they said no. It was a *quarter*! You can't destroy my life and my dreams and make me sad and miserable because of what you say. I've already heard my worst no. There is no "no" on earth worse than that.

Since then I've never been afraid to try new things. I've never been afraid of the unknown, because I didn't understand most of the stuff around me. I didn't know what was going on in my life and it removed that fear. When you're desperate to get out of your situation, you'll pretty much do anything to change or improve your circumstances. My upbringing and what I was exposed to removed that fear of rejection. I pray for you that you're not in a situation like the one I was growing up in. But as I've said before, sometimes you've got to go through the fire to realize what you're in and get to that better place, whatever that may be for you.

Don't concern yourself with somebody else's opinion of what you're supposed to do with your life and how you're supposed to dress and how you're supposed to go about your life. Some of the most successful people in the world are some of the weirdest, the oddest—the opposite of whatever "cool" is—because they're very into their own thing and their comfort zone and their world. Look at Bill Gates. He doesn't remind me of a guy who has danced on top of tables, spraying champagne, wilding out like a star football player. He's a geeky guy, but he's still cool as hell because he discovered his love, he discovered his passion, he discovered the things that moved him and intrigued him, and he was comfortable with being weird, comfortable with being different.

Get comfortable in your weird. Get comfortable in your different thoughts. Get comfortable in who you are and the things that you're into. Just because other people out there might not connect and they might call you weird and spooky and kooky, that's all right! Think of it this way: You could transform yourself into a happier, more positive person. You could be the next CEO of a Fortune 500 company because you decided to stay comfortable in your different thoughts, and all these other dudes are going to be begging to work for you. Just ask Steve Jobs and Mark Zuckerberg.

If you don't believe in yourself it may be because you're surrounding yourself with negative people who make you think you couldn't be any of those things or make those changes in your life. You need to find your own direction, be your own person, and not be ashamed of who you are. The only reason to not do it is if you're afraid of the unknown. I decided I was going to spread my wings and try everything possible because I didn't know if only one thing would get me to the top. So do your own thing. Elevate yourself to the top.

As soon as you decide what you want to do with your life, your family and your friends and the people in your immediate life may be the first people to try and talk you out of your goals. It doesn't always happen that you'll tell someone how you want to change your life and they get into a full-on display of support, enthusiasm, and encouragement for you to keep going, even helping you with the execution of your thoughts. It does happen, but in most cases, as soon as you decide, or God sends you a confirmation that this is what you're supposed to do and this is a new chapter that you're supposed to begin, the people in your immediate circle, the people who are in your life, are the first ones to try and discourage you out of that plan.

Ideas Are Blessings

When these ideas and these messages and this game plan is sent to you, it is sent to you for a reason. Every time you get an idea it's a blessing from God.

I believe the two closest experiences to God are water and ideas. Think of it this way: Your body is made of 90 percent water. Most of the world is made of water. The liquid in your body is red, but it's still liquid. Liquid in your eyes helps you blink, the liquid in your mouth helps you break down food. When you have a child, your baby starts out as a form of liquid. And when you get an idea, you're closer to God, because like Him, you're creating something for the world and for yourself. You're channeling God's idea, something that He sent to you. And God would never give you something somebody else is supposed to have.

Don't rob the world of what you're thinking. Don't rob the world of your ideas and your plans, because everything in your life, every material and physical thing, every building, every piece of furniture, every new technology, everything that you see, was somebody's thoughts. And these people decided to execute those thoughts and get them out and allow their thoughts to be materialized, and that's why we are now *experiencing* what somebody else thought. I was at a restaurant one night having a business meeting, and the restaurant was so beautiful—its design and architecture, everything from the food to the outfits the servers were wearing—and then it hit me: I was sitting *inside* somebody's idea! My brain started going further and I started looking at every little thing, realizing that every aspect of this restaurant was first in someone's mind and then it became physical, something *real*. And I wondered if I was tripping—because I don't drink and I don't smoke, so the stuff I come up with kind of hits me throughout the day. But this was valuable to me. We are always *experiencing* someone else's idea. Since then I have never looked at the things around me the same way.

I want you to stop for a quick second and look around. Are you reading this book at a table or sitting on a train? Are you on an airplane? Wherever you are, you're sitting at or sitting inside somebody's thoughts while you're reading this book. If you're in a car, somebody thought of how to make the car, and design the car. But if they had kept those ideas in their mind, you would have never been able to purchase the car.

When you walk around a city and you look at the architecture, and you're thinking how beautiful the buildings are, you're looking at somebody's thoughts. That building, as big as it is, was inside of somebody's mind and they were able to get it out and make it physical—and now you're standing in someone's idea. People are working or living inside somebody's thoughts. So don't rob the world of what you're thinking. Get it out. You don't have to be a brainiac. If you ever want to create something, just go for it. I want to experience what you're thinking. You can make the world better with your ideas.

So my question becomes, What are your designs? What are your ideas? Why *wouldn't* you want the world to experience your thoughts and ideas? Haven't there been times when you had an idea to do something or invent something and then a couple years go by and some product comes out and you think, *Damn, I thought of that forever ago!* The thing is, you didn't execute. So what happens is—and this is my own theory: God sends you the idea first, but you're lazy. You may tell people about it, you may write it down, but you don't execute it to the point of bringing this thought and idea to life, and so He sends it to somebody else. It could be an idea for anything—to invent something, design something, a way you can change your life.

If you don't have a high school diploma, or you never went to college, or you dropped out, you may feel discouraged when you want to get your ideas out. There are plenty of multimillionaires who didn't graduate from high school or college. Now, I'm not encouraging you to drop out of school, because school brings education, opportunities, and connections. I'm just saying that you don't need to have degrees in order to execute your ideas and plans. Experience is your highest truth. To me, experience is the highest level of education. Are you a singer, songwriter, or music producer? Do you have film ideas, or want to write screenplays, or become a film director? I've learned that if I surround myself with people who are the things I want to become, at some point I will become them.

Don't rob the world of what you're thinking. Get it out. Execute. When you have an idea, stop telling people all your business, because in most cases people are not happy for you. Stop telling people your business, stop talking so much. Be a silent force. Stop talking and looking for affirmation from everybody. We all get excited about our ideas and we want to share them with our friends and family, our circle. But not everybody is going to see what you see and if they don't, they may try and talk you out of executing your ideas. If the Wright brothers told their friends about their idea for an airplane and people laughed at them, if they had kept that idea in their minds, we wouldn't be flying around the world on airplanes. If Dr. King had kept his interpretation of the way he saw the world in his mind, then we wouldn't be living in the country that we live in, in the world we live in now. He had an idea of how the world should be and was determined to make it happen, even if it killed him. And then slowly but surely it started happening.

Salvador Dali said, "Geniuses must never die. The progress of mankind depends on us." The first time I heard that quote it messed me up because it's *true*. We won't progress without genius or ideas. Everything you do, and everywhere you go, you're experiencing somebody's thoughts. Everything is somebody's idea. So the questions become, What do you think? What do you want for yourself? What are your ideas? What is your *purpose*? You are so important to the progress of mankind, so much more important than you think. You have thoughts and ideas running in your mind.

Most people believe you have to be famous to change the world, but I disagree with that. As a matter of fact, there are a lot of people that I know whose lives are miserable because of fame. They feel isolated, like they have to hide from the world. They can't just wake up and decide to go to the mall because they'll never make it through one store. There have been a few moments where I've personally hated fame because my privacy was violated, or certain rumors were spread about me. There have been a few different occasions when I've walked down the street with guys worth millions; one time, people walked up to us, asked me for my autograph and then asked the billionaire I was with to take the picture! I was smiling while my friend took the picture and the whole time I was thinking, *Wow, I wish I were on the other side of this camera. This guy is able to walk down the street in peace. He's a multimillionaire, he's a game changer, running a successful business, but he doesn't have paparazzi following him home or any of the issues that come with being a celeb.* Of course this guy is famous within his own world and circle, but the average Joe wouldn't know who he was. I'll never forget one time my former manager Greg Parks, who discovered me, told me, "Tyrese, I wouldn't want to be you. I got the best of both worlds. I can be around you and all this madness, screams, and energy, and then two days later I can be in the mall shopping and be completely ignored and anonymous. You can't cut it off and decide tomorrow you don't want to be famous anymore, but I can. All I have to do is decide to not hang out with you and nobody will give me that attention."

Even if you don't have fame and fortune you can still execute because there is value in your *relationships*—more value than what you may have in the bank. I am sure President Obama still has some friends that grew up with him who may only have a couple thousand dollars in their bank account, but they have the president's cell phone number. I wouldn't think anything less of President Obama's friend because of the amount of money he doesn't have because he has the relationship and direct access to the president of the United States. There is more value in every relationship you have. Whether you're rich or poor, if you maintain your relationships, you can still execute your ideas.

I can't tell you enough: You are that genius. There doesn't have to be any difference between you and Oprah Winfrey and Barack Obama. Obama had an idea of how he saw himself, that he could be president, and he stopped at nothing until he was able to make that thought and idea that God put in his heart a reality. I want you to understand that you have that power, you have that force, you have that idea waiting to materialize, but you must be in a positive frame of mind to transform your thoughts from just an idea into a physical reality.

You should expect a lot of people to say no. But don't get discouraged, because when one door closes, it means that that door wasn't for you, or that could mean that the timing for your idea wasn't right. Sean Diddy Combs told me that Benny Medina, who used to manage him, had at least twelve to fifteen different meetings about getting Diddy's clothing line off the ground. At first nobody got it. They met with all the heavyweights, but they weren't feeling it. Years later, we know that hundreds of millions of dollars were made from Sean John clothing. And now, people will meet with any new client that Benny Medina brings to the table. In that world, money and revenue are what's associated with being successful. There was something about what Benny and Diddy saw from the beginning that these other folks didn't see. But they kept at it and became a huge success. So don't rob the world of what you're thinking.

Fall in Love with Your Ideas

At the beginning of this book, I told you about how I had to fall in love with myself and the idea of what I wanted to become. Well, the same should apply to you. People used to always say to me, "Where do you come up with all of this stuff, man?" At some point I started thinking I was a weirdo when it came to some of my ideas and my perspective on life. I had to fall in love with who I was all over again, so that I could be more comfortable with who I am and not feel like I needed to go out of my way to try and impress somebody or be on the same page as *everybody* I met. With more self-love I was able to achieve the impossible.

I've never been competitive, I've never been motivated to outdo, be bigger than, or be better than others. I've always wanted to be the best version of *me*. When other people are doing really well, and they're maximizing their area of expertise, they motivate me and inspire me, but I'm not on a mission to take them out. I think when people are on a mission to take someone out, or outdo them, or beat them, there is always a level of condescension connected with competition. Your insecurity can make you think negatively, and that negativity infests everything. If you're saying *They're not better than me*, that's degrading and condescending in its own way. You just have to remember that God would never give you something somebody else is supposed to have. If you're competing with someone, like in a boxing match, and you both have the same gloves and both trained your asses off, at the end of the day, whoever is going to win this match is who God had intended to win the match. You gave it your all, I gave it my all. It's in God's hands. But that doesn't mean you should not try.

You want to be inspired to reach for more because you've been exposed to someone doing it on a higher level. In the same way, like my friend Brandy Norwood once told me, *You'll never know who you are till you discover who you're not.* You have to be secure with who you are and what you've done and what you're doing so that you can be happy for other people to have what they have. In the same way, if you don't achieve something— for whatever reason—you know more about yourself and you can overcome other hurdles once you have clarity on that.

Get your self-confidence together, in order to focus on what you really want to do. The first thing that you have to do is to fall in love with yourself. If you're going to be depressed and full of self-hatred, then you're not going to get anything accomplished.

You have to not only fall in love with yourself, you also have to fall in love with your own ideas. Because when you do, no one will be able to talk you out of them. Fall in love with your idea—whatever it is. An idea is something that you want to create for *yourself.* It could be an idea *of* yourself.

I have a friend from the United Arab Emirates. There are a lot of restrictions in her culture, they have all of these laws and rules for women because it's a very strict traditional country. But she decided that she wanted to reinvent the wheel and not be like a lot of the other women in her community. She wanted to go and actually see the world, to see what's out there. Even though she knew she was going to bump her head a few times here and there, she wanted to get out there and really see what the world is about, because she knew there had to be so much more than what was in her own country. She wanted to experience the freedom of being able to do what she wants, when she wants, where she wants, and with whom she wants. She had to fall in love with her *idea* of how she sees her life and what she wanted to do with her life. And the day that she fell in love with her idea, no one could talk her out of what she wanted to do. Even though she made some bad choices along the way and she sounded regretful at times, overall she has no regrets about leaving her country and seeing what the world is about. The concept of falling in love with yourself and falling in love with your own ideas can also mean falling in love with the way you decide how you want to live *your* life.

See the Impossible

Blindness is a handicap that some are born with and others get along the way. Ray Charles was blind and Stevie Wonder is blind—these are geniuses of our time who literally can't see. And yet, we can consider them *visionaries* when it comes to music! On several occasions I had the honor of hanging out with Stevie Wonder. One night in his dressing room after a show, I asked him, "If you had your choice, would you want to see?" And he told me that he didn't want to see because his life is as amazing as it is even without seeing the things that people are able to see with their eyes. He doesn't have any mental *pictures* in his mind, all he has is his experience and his own thoughts. Stevie can't be distracted by visual images streaming in front of him. What he experiences physically is the only memory he has. He doesn't know what I look like but he told me he enjoyed my *energy* and presence and I was honored when he told me he considers me a friend.

Stevie's discernment and his instincts and his intuition as a man who can't see is a different experience and makes me wonder how most of us have been blessed to be able to see and use our eyes physically, but we can't envision better lives for ourselves. We have the physical ability to see, but we're still blind. A lot of our bad choices are considered *blind* choices. When your people get mad and disgusted with you and your actions and your choices they always make reference to vision and the visual—*You had to be blind to not see that that dude was not good for you. You had to be blind to not see that what you're putting your-self through is not good.* Some people can't *see* that they should want better for themselves. They have the convenience of being able to see with their own eyes, but they decide to stay blind. I want you to take the blinders off and try to see the invisible. I want you to dream with your eyes open.

This is America, land of the free. This is America, a land of opportunity. Some people in other countries would cut off their left arm to be here because they can make money and provide for their families. You live here and maybe you haven't done anything, maybe you're just sitting back and doing nothing. But this is America. You can finish high school, go to college, get a job. All you have to do is show up to make something happen. There is no excuse for anyone to not try and move their life forward. There is so much you can do, why don't you see it?

One night I was watching the news and back to back there were all these negative stories about random crimes, murders, break-ins, and carjackings. It made me think that some people take all the opportunities and access we have in America for granted. Some people are just sitting at home, not even trying to find a job or do anything to change their circumstances or situation; they just freeload and collect unemployment, social security, and other kinds of free money. For some reason on this particular night I had a random, extreme idea to create an exchange program where I would take a hundred dysfunctional American people overseas to a country in the middle of nowhere, where everything is isolated and regular people barely make money, and live in poverty, struggle for food, and don't have the access, power, or control—a place where people are bound to their lifestyle so even if they try to do something different they are just stuck. I would then bring a hundred people from the same poor country to America for a year and see how they would take pure advantage of all the amazing things that we have access to in this country. I can almost guarantee that these people would have multiple flourishing careers compared to the hundred Americans that would be sent overseas. Once the Americans came home, after living in huts, making seven to twelve cents a day, and having no access, money, or power—maybe even having to hunt for their food—they'd appreciate America so much more.

People who have been in America for two or three years have said to me, "Americans are lazy. They have no idea how blessed they are to be in this country. I am in America to take advantage of all the gold that's under everyone's noses that no one is making use of." There should be no such thing as poverty in America when you have this much access. It's the only place where you can go from being homeless to being a millionaire within the same year if you just make the right choices. Unless someone is mentally challenged or has a debilitating handicap there is no reason to be unemployed or not trying to do something creative to get something off the ground. This is America, the land of opportunity. Many people don't know how good we really have it. I know there's a recession and the unemployment rate in this country is at an all-time high, but I'm also aware that there are people out there who were capable of working *before* the recession hit, who purposely decided to be lazy bums and sit around the house collecting unemployment and taking advantage of the system.

You have to believe in yourself. Don't allow your friends and family to discourage you from what you're thinking. It all goes back to self-love. You are not a Siamese twin. Your heart and mind are not connected to anyone else's because God blessed us with individual minds. You are so much more than you can ever imagine. If God was done with you, you wouldn't be here anymore. What is the mission you are supposed to be living out? Everyone has a purpose. God has a purpose for our being here. It's not too late to figure out what you want for yourself.

The beauty of thinking and coming up with your ideas for yourself along the way is that your story and your thoughts are always evolving. You change, you transition, you're on your way to another level. You're on the ladder and you're heading up to that place where your better you is. Every little bit of knowledge and self-love you gain is another rung of the ladder that brings you closer to that better place. I hope that by giving people some knowledge and information about what's around the corner I will somehow make getting up the ladder a bit easier.

Chapter 8

Are You Ready for the Next Level?

When you come up with an idea—a purpose—you have to set a plan in motion for how you're going to *execute* your idea.

When it comes to execution, the thing that I specialize in is a Things to Do List. My Things to Do List is for both my personal and business lives. I write down everything. My lists are thorough, detailed—they could go up to a hundred pages. I will walk through my house with a pen and a pad and will write down everything that needs to get done, or I will sit down in front of a laptop and go through everything I can think of. I type the whole thing out and then I'll cut and paste it into a regular e-mail and send it to people who work with me. After that I'll follow up with everyone some time later.

One time I was on a flight, thirteen hours overseas, and I went through my phone and wrote a list of reminders of things I was supposed to follow up on or execute for every name in my phone. I could more than likely figure out *something* pertaining to each person in my phone right now because they wouldn't be in my contacts if they weren't important or relevant in my life.

It's all part of the hustle: I wouldn't be in this position if I were not supposed to maximize the stage that I've been blessed to stand on. Your career and your life is that stage. You wouldn't be blessed to know or have access to the people you have access to if you weren't supposed to figure out a way to make use of those relationships. There is a *reason* every single person has been brought into your life and your journey.

So get organized and execute your dream!

Do You Own the Blessing?

Before you even start executing your plan, you have to feel like you *own* the blessing. When you own the blessing, you work really hard to maintain it. But if you feel like you don't own it—if it's something you feel you don't deserve or even asked for—most likely you won't work hard to keep it. The reason a lot of people suffer from self-sabotage and self-defeat and don't work hard to maintain the blessing is because they don't feel like it's really theirs.

When I first started singing, my only motivation to get out of the hood was survival—I didn't want to be hungry anymore. Once I wasn't hungry and was making money, something in me was making me underperform. I wasn't working nearly as hard as I had in the beginning of my career. I got complacent and lazy and was sabotaging a lot of the good things going on in my life. The world didn't see it that way, but as new opportunities came my way I would figure out a way to bring some dysfunction into a situation that wasn't dysfunctional at all.

It was like I was enjoying this successful life on borrowed time, and at some point the clock would strike midnight and the coach would turn back into a pumpkin, like in *Cinderella*. It felt like everything was so unreal because it happened so fast: I went from extreme nothingness and dysfunction and craziness to the extreme opposite of that very quickly—success, bling, good food.

I was sabotaging my blessings because I didn't feel I owned them. I was afraid I would lose everything. I knew I was going to be a singer but the modeling and acting were unexpected blessings I didn't *ask* for. I took them for granted and I didn't protect them. Even though I worked my ass off to get where I was, once it started happening I felt like somebody was going to pinch me or wake me up and tell me my run was over. I felt like the blessings were rented, like my career was a rental car. Think about how you treat a rental car compared to how you treat your own car—you're burning rubber, sometimes you lock the door and sometimes you don't. But if the car is yours, you treat it with respect and decency; you wouldn't put cheap gas in a car that belongs to you. If you treat your life, the people around you, or your house, like a rental car, then the blessing is going to go away.

Since I felt like it was going to end anyway, I figured I would end it myself. That way I could control the way it would end. I would have done it to myself instead of someone completely taking it away from me. I actually found myself being negative about so many things that were so positive and so wonderful—I didn't want to accept all the great things in my life if they were going to disappear. That was a very negative mind-set to have.

I had to recognize the blessing and I had to take owner-ship of it. This blessing was *mine*, and I had to take care of it and take responsibility for it and continue to hustle. I had to become the master of my environment and *believe* it.

We often want more than we have, but we should own the blessing, own what we have now, and maintain it. We have to work harder at maintaining the blessing. Uphold it like it's your last, and act like it's not going to be there tomorrow.

Do you own the blessing? The more you appreciate the unexpected blessings, everything you are asking for and trying to accomplish will reveal itself eventually. The more you love yourself and know that you *do* deserve your blessings, the more you will be ready for the next level.

Figure out if you're committed and willing to do the work. Commit to your goal. Commitment is knowing how far you are willing to go to get to where you're destined to be. So many people believe they know where they should be in their minds, but they are not as willing to put in the work to get there. Are you willing to make the commitment just to get to the highest level you can? You've got to protect your blessings and do the work. My mentor John Bryant told me that *Success is going from failure to failure without loss of enthusiasm.* You have to be enthusiastic to stay on your path—and you need self-love and respect to execute the idea and maintain the blessing.

You also have to understand your motives. Are they financial? Are you just hoping to buy stuff you don't have? When I talk about *ideas* I don't just mean ideas for making money, but ideas for getting to your better place, whatever that may be. Money will not make you happy. Everyone who is broke and wishes they had more money is assuming life will be better with money. Some people say *mo' money mo' problems*, but I think having more money with the *wrong people* in your life is what brings more problems. When you have more money and you have great people in your life, then you're able to enjoy all the fruits of life that come from having money. Material things will not make you happy, especially if you have a lot of dysfunction in your life. You have to clear away the dysfunction and make more room for self-love. Dysfunction makes being broke even worse and it doesn't let you enjoy the success, either. Sure it's a pleasure to have certain things, but it's not the be-all and end-all to your happiness.

A few years ago I was in my Bentley—I'm not being flashy, I work hard. I was at the light at Crenshaw and Slauson, and I was *miserable*. It had been a crazy couple of months for me, and I was sad and broken down. I was at the light and I saw this dude at the bus stop with some headphones on, dancing and having the time of his life. I was thinking, *Look at this guy with the headphones on, in the hood, happy as a mofo, and I'm sitting in a Bentley all miserable.* I actually said to myself, *I wish I was that dude at the bus stop.* I had dropped all this cash for the sound system and the car and that dude just had headphones and bus fare, and he was happier than me.

There are still times when I have to remind myself that I'm the master of my environment, despite my success. It's one thing to say you're the master of your environment, and it's another thing for you to actually *believe* it and *act* upon it. I could say to people hundreds of times that I'm the master of my environment, but if I don't believe it, then it's not really the case.

Every Level's Another Devil

Every level's another Devil means that as you reach and try to grow, the Devil will get busy and try to distract you from bettering yourself. A friend of mine told this to me when he was going through some heavy stuff and I never forgot it. I identified with it because even after achieving success I still had to deal with a lot of dysfunction. The Devil creates obstacles to get you off focus from your goals. The Devil will try and get you to go back to your old ways. The more you try to love yourself is when the Devil is going to come at you, so you've got to try your best to ignore those negative thoughts—stay strong and stay focused.

When you get to the big opportunity, the Devil comes back at you stronger because you have more responsibility, people want more from you, and you have more to lose. You're out and about trying to figure things out and one thing is happening after another and as soon as that big thing happens, that's when everybody rushes toward you, everybody's aggressively trying to get your attention. With every new step comes another obstacle you've got to overcome. Don't let yourself get discouraged. If you've come this far you've got to remind yourself that you can go farther.

I can still get discouraged—as a father, an ex-husband, boyfriend, friend, son, actor, or singer. I think everyone gets discouraged when they don't get something they want really bad, especially if they want something and don't know why they didn't get it. I get discouraged working out because I don't love to do it. I remind myself of my blessings and get back to self-love to stay fired up.

We associate God with good, and the Devil with bad, but one time my security guard's mother told me something interesting. She said we have a bad habit of giving the Devil credit. If something goes bad, we say the Devil did it. When we do that, we're technically *praising* the Devil for his work and giving him credit. This wonderful woman said we should never even recognize or give the Devil opportunity for praise. We shouldn't even make reference to the Devil and act like the Devil doesn't exist. But sometimes we have to be *aware* that he's out there to stay on our game. Don't allow the Devil to lure you away from focusing on your goals.

People say idle time is the Devil's playground. They end up doing stupid things when they're bored that they wouldn't do if they were busy—things they will regret later—I know I definitely have. If you're not advancing your life in a personal or professional way, you're opening yourself up to doing things you won't be proud of.

I've said this before, but it's arrogant to believe the next second belongs to you. Now, when I said that earlier, it was about abusive relationships and how your life could change or end in one second. But it's also about your life and what you want from your life. Because I've seen it—growing up in the hood, with people dying all around me—your life can change in one second. So take that second to make the decision about how you're going to get to that better place.

Setbacks

There will be times when you'll be forced to take a step backward. The key to getting out of these situations is remembering what your bottom line is *while* you are moving backward. In other words, always keep sight of your goal. As long as your step backward is connected to trying to achieve your goal, you don't have anything to worry about. Think about it as a challenge that God wants you to face an opportunity head-on and to prove to yourself and Him that you are strong enough to overcome it.

The problems arise when your setback is caused by allowing your bottom line to shift—like if you allow a person to suck you back into dysfunction.

It's hard if you're in the spirit of being discouraged and wanting to give up. Bishop Ulmer once told me that when we go through setbacks, *God is setting us back to set us up.* He's got something special planned out for us. Bishop Ulmer explained it like this: God is a quarterback. In football, a quarterback takes the ball and draws back a few steps, and then throws the ball for a touchdown. Life is like that sometimes. You've got to draw back in order to throw as far as you can to get the touchdown. Even when you go backward, you've got to keep your bottom line in mind, and not go back to that man or woman or friend who brought you misery. Stay off the pity potty, get back to self-love.

I look at my life for the blessing it is, and you've got to fight for your blessings. You can't give up because it's not happening as fast as you want. Don't give up on college or high school because it's tough and your teacher or coach is giving you a hard time. You have to *fight*. If you want to respark your careers, do what you have to do to educate yourself, surround yourself with better people who will support you, and don't let the ideas die because of the circumstances you fell into. There are still things I want to accomplish. I want to go back to school and get my degree in filmmaking, to become a director and a better writer and an expert on the whole film process. I'm still in the process of executing that goal.

I keep my spirit open to allow people to come in my life and elevate me, because I'm constantly on a mission to be the best version of me. When I'm given options for how to do something I always take time to assess which way would be best. If there's anything I don't understand, I reach out to the people I have in my life. If I can't come up with an answer or make a decision on anything I'm going through, I'll at least put it out there and see if someone says something that makes sense for me so I can make the best decision. A lot of times we are in our own way because we're not able to come up with the best scenario or the best answer for ourselves. Sometimes our own ideas are not the best ways to deal with a problem or a situation, or sometimes we're so in our own minds and need that other point of view to shake up our approach to fixing our problem and help us get to a better place in our lives.

I want you to initiate your career and get to your better place. Stay in that space of self-love and be a person of integrity. Do not put your beliefs on the line to get your career off the ground because God is watching. It's not only about what you're capable of, it's about whom you know. Relationships are everything. Get off your ass and hustle.

Open your mind and spirit. I know I can hit somebody with advice, and people will have a legitimate response that they are not able to do anything beyond their existing circumstances. I know it won't be easy for some people to change their environment. But I hope reading this book will change your mind-set and help you realize that with most situations in your life, if you're staying in those circumstances or that environment, it's something you're *choosing* to do. If you want better for yourself, seek out people who can help you or inspire you to change your circumstances.

I hope you'll see that where there's a will, there's a way, and once you take that first step, you may go through a rough patch and be down in the middle of the pit, but at some point there will be a light at the end of that tunnel, and when you see that light you better run, run fast as you can, and never turn back.

The Art of the Hustle

A hustle can take many forms, and it doesn't necessarily have to be a bad thing. It's just about trying to make something out of nothing any way you can and maximizing your potential. The hustle has created opportunities for me. That's why I was able to take a thirty-second commercial and turn it into a fifteen-year career in show business. I give myself credit for hustling. I believe in you and I believe you have what it takes. There's nothing you can't do. The only limits are the ones you create for yourself.

You have to focus on the big picture and have a vision of where you're going and where you want to be. I've always been bold but for a long time it was just sporadic. In my personal life and career, I was bold with no sense of direction.

In fact, my movie career started as one of those random bold moves. It wasn't part of my plans to start in music and transition into movies. I didn't want anything to do with Hollywood, movies, none of that. But if you want to make God laugh, you tell Him your plans.

John Singleton will tell the story of how we first met. I was seventeen or eighteen and at a random Hollywood event, and John was there. Everybody knew him from *Boyz n the Hood* and *Poetic Justice*. Everybody knew he was a talented young black director from South Central and we all knew he had worked with Tupac. John says I walked right up to him at this party and said something like *I'm a movie star and I'm gonna work with you one day.* He was just like *Okay, whatever!* I don't remember doing it, I don't remember saying it. But he does and he's told the story a few times.

Years went by, and I ran into John a few more times. He was basically watching me grow up in the business, selling records, doing videos, my Guess campaign, hosting for MTV. He was directing *Shaft* and he wanted me to be in it, but I basically told him no. At the time, I wasn't interested in doing anything in Hollywood. I was just so focused on my music career, being on the road and having fun with it, and I couldn't wrap my head around anything that had to do with Hollywood. The other thing was that I came from the hood. I was dealing with the pressures of people saying *You're acting real Hollywood*, and worrying that people were thinking I'd gotten this attitude that I was successful and had made it. Whether you're successful in movies or music, they still say you went Hollywood when you start acting all arrogant. I *really* didn't want to be seen like that, and if I were in the movies, my boys could definitely say I went all Hollywood. Looking back I know that was stupid, because I was making money from music anyway. But I was young.

John was in New York working on *Shaft* and he was blowing up my phone, trying to get me to do the movie. I eventually changed my number because I knew how powerful he was and I didn't want to keep telling him *no.* I can go on record that John Singleton is one of the first people to see something in me that I didn't see in myself.

I kept avoiding John, but once I saw the movie *Hurricane*, with Denzel Washington, stepping up was a no-brainer for me. I wanted to do what Denzel had done, so I said yes to the role of Jody in *Baby Boy*. Tupac was supposed to play the part of Jody but John offered it to me after Tupac died. I met up with John at the first house I ever bought and he was so tough because I had been avoiding him. We were sitting at the dinner table and he was telling me these different things he wanted to do in the movie, but I hadn't read the script yet. He was basically pitching the movie to me and painting the picture—all the conflicts between the character I would play and Ving Rhames's character and my mama and baby mamas and the tension at home from being a grown man living at home—and I thought, *This guy is describing my life!*

John started reading a few pages and then said, *Fuck this, you read it!* I sat there and read the whole script, right in front of him. I didn't really have to figure out the intricacies of what was going on between the characters because I had lived through a lot of that, except having children, of course. Even though that role was like a custom suit and John wanted me and had basically given me the role, I still felt like I had a lot to prove. I asked him if I could audition.

I went to the Linwood Swap Meet in the hood, bought a beanie, a huge T-shirt, some Dickies, and some Chuck Taylors and went to the audition *as* Baby Boy. I felt like I wanted to earn the role. I wanted to confirm what I was feeling—that I wasn't sure if I wanted to do this movie thing, but I needed to try and I wanted to figure it out. John already knew I had it in me but I still wanted to *show* him that I had it.

When the movie wrapped I said I was never going to act again, and I didn't do a movie after that for a couple of years. I went back to my music full-time because, for the most part, music wasn't as challenging for me. *Baby Boy* had been so heavy; I was working with an acting coach, Michelle Richards, but more than that, I had to stay in a dark space for the entire shoot, which was difficult for me. I had finally been out of the hood, traveling, moving around, having a career, and those three months on set were a constant reminder of my childhood. They were tremendously draining.

After *Baby Boy* I was getting plenty of movie offers. Everybody was buzzing about my performance. Once again my life had completely changed. I couldn't wrap my head around it all, it wasn't real for me yet. I remember thinking to myself, *Wow, this is some real Hollywood shit.* I had never gone through that before and didn't really believe they were complimenting me. Instead of going in a new direction, I jumped back on the road.

A couple years later *2 Fast 2 Furious* came up. The offer was totally beyond any amount I had heard before and I really didn't have to think about that; I took the job right away. John Singleton got me my first movie in Hollywood, and I got John Singleton *2 Fast 2 Furious*. I had gone into a meeting and the original director wasn't coming back for the sequel. I said, "John Singleton would be *incredible* doing the movie," and that's how it happened. That was my first experience making connections between people.

Back then, making that connection wasn't a strategy of any sort. Even after John signed on, I didn't realize that was the reason he'd gotten the job, because at the time they never suggested they would hire him. Besides, he was already John Singleton. Now, making connections for me is very strategic and well thought-out. It does something for me to know that two talented or capable people are putting their energy, thoughts, and ideas together and trying to move it into something. I'm a connector. I like connecting people and situations and seeing what will happen. When I think two people will get along based on their personalities or interests, I don't always think about how it will benefit me or that I will be a part of their projects. I just get a kick out of making things happen.

Before, I had been hustling, I had been bold, but I never had a strategy. Now, I'm the guy that thinks about *everything*. My days of winging it are over. There should be only a few opportunities that come by that I don't think about first. Now I know when I need to plant a seed. I consider that *masterminding*.

There are a lot of people who are bold and confident and have the audacity and just step in, but you have to ask yourself, *What are you stepping into?* What are you arranging? You can boldly step your ass into the circle but what are you going to do when you get there? I had been bold with no sense of direction. I had walked up to John Singleton and told him I was going to be in one of his movies, but now I am bold with a sense of *vision*.

You have to come up with a plan. You're either winging it or you're strategizing. What's the plan? What's the next level? What are your thoughts? You want to allow the world to experience your thoughts because they mean nothing if they stay in your mind. Your intentions mean nothing if they stay in your heart.

It took me some time to jump full-on into the movie game. My intentions were to take my movie money and help further my music career. Originally my heart was not in acting. But ultimately, I got to a place where I had to stop fighting the inevitability of what was right in front of me. I had to think about how many records I have sold. I've done well, but I haven't sold the substantial amount of records that other young fly black dudes have sold. People love my voice, and love what I do as a singer, and women show up to see me in concert, but I haven't reached the level of other successful music stars. I'm not trying to devalue myself, but I was fighting and fighting trying to do music even when everything about movies to me is so first-class and heavyweight. I realize now that I was fighting God's plan and the benefits He was bringing to me by helping me get these movie roles.

I had to be honest and come clean with myself. I may never be the biggest music star in the world. There is a possibility that that is ultimately not in the cards, so what am I going to do? I decided to maximize every possible opportunity and try to ride it out to its full potential. That is my responsibility, my duty and my priority.

I was spinning my wheels in the music industry. You've got to go to the gym and shoot a video and go on the road and do concerts and radio promotions. You have to pay for all the dancers and the band and the travel—*everything*. Financially I was not benefiting as well as I could have been, compared to acting.

People were reaching out to me with movie roles and I was running away from them, trying to chase a music career. What was I doing? It was completely asinine for anybody to say their first love is music when they're down here financially at the end of the day, and everything about the movies puts them in a better bracket. I believe in sacrifice. I believe in the balls-out, all-or-nothing approach to getting things done but I also believe in common sense. My common sense told me this: If I'm on the road, I'm going to have two tour buses, which are going to cost a lot of money—I have to pay for the gas, the driver, my band, the rental equipment, their salaries, the dancers, all their costumes, the hotels that we're going to stay in. I was giving up 20 percent to my management, another 10 percent to the booking agent who booked the shows, and all of the other random expenses that may come up, like last-minute emergency flights; whatever it was, I had to take care of it, because it was my tour. Of course, as you work your way up the ranks, the guys booking you for the shows, the promoters, will cover a lot of your expenses just to make sure you actually come and do their show, and right before I tapped out of the music game there were some expenses that the promoters covered for me. But pretty much everything else was on me.

Could I disregard the experience, could I say I didn't love my fans and people singing along with me and screaming my name? Could I say I didn't love every moment of being on stage, listening to my fans sing along with my songs and come to my after-parties? No, I couldn't say that. But at the end of the tour, after doing three or four or five in a row, it became very clear to me that financially I was more in the red than in the black. More money was going out to put the tour together than what was coming in. Some managers or agents or lawyers can look at my breakdown and say just maybe Tyrese had bad advisers. I could beg to differ, but that's neither here nor there.

Here's the Hollywood breakdown. When I do films, I make

millions of dollars. I have to give up 10 percent to my agency, 5 percent to my lawyer, I pay my taxes, and then everything else is mine. In the movie game they don't say *We're going to pay you and then after the movie comes out you're going to owe us the money we paid you to be in the movie until the movie earns back its budget.* In the music game you get an advance that goes to your pocket. You also get an album budget that goes to pay for your producers, your studio, your travel expenses, and the rental equipment that you may use while you're working on your masterpiece. But all the money you're spending that they gave you in advance has to be earned back—paid back to the label—by selling albums, and only when it is do you start to make royalties. To me the music industry business model is the highest level of pimping I've ever experienced in my life.

Here are more Hollywood details: They pay me to be in their movie. When the movie comes out, they have a budget of several thousand dollars to pay for my expenses for a stylist, hair, and wardrobe, all my travel is first-class, including private jets, to whatever city we're filming in, or doing press junkets in. During filming they pay for my trainer, my living expenses, and they rent me a car of my choice. *None* of this money has to be paid back to them, so it's all upside. Of course, we have to do interviews to help promote the movie during the press junket, but all of the marketing and advertising that goes for the movie is also at their expense, and if the movie doesn't end up doing well, that's on them. Obviously, if you're associated with a film that doesn't do well it leans on your name, but whether you signed up to do a bad movie or not, as an actor you just have to show up and give your best performance; people could say they didn't like the overall movie, but at least your performance was solid. Some actors get back-end bonuses when a movie does really well. For example, if your movie grosses $100 million—or whatever your contract states—the studio sends you a bonus check.

I have some unfortunate news for you music fans out there: A lot of your favorite singers and rappers aren't as passionate about music as they used to be when they first started because of the lack of money that's being made in the industry. Part of this is because of the Internet and free or illegal sharing of music files, and some online companies take huge percentages of each album sold. Because some rap stars and musicians have no other business options, they're just going into the studio and put out albums they're not passionate about just so they can survive and pay their bills. I believe it's because of this that some music has been watered down and doesn't have nearly as much soul as it did back in the day.

I'm giving you all these details because your first love and what you're really passionate about can sometimes bring a harsh reality for your finances. If you have the option to do something else that will help you earn money, I recommend you secure your future financially. When you do, you will be able to focus on the things you're really passionate about without depending on the things you're passionate about to pay your bills.

You should *always be strategizing*. Don't be another successful businessman or -woman who goes from being worth a few thousand dollars to millions of dollars and doesn't know how to properly invest their money. Someone once told me that the biggest problem for most people who make a lot of money is that they are not aware or prepared for when they have reached their peak. Imagine if a boxer is making ten or fifteen million dollars a fight. Everything about his lifestyle represents that money, but he doesn't know that he earned his last ten or fifteen million. He keeps thinking that his career is still going to continue and that another ten million will be coming to him, so his spending habits and his overhead are way over the top. He's not in the mind-set to save and didn't know that he just received his last check. We hear about it all the time: injuries and unexpected situations come up, so you've got to have emergency money off to the side, because you never know when you've reached your peak.

Whether you're a boxer, or a football or corporate player, you must always be aware of the next step and the possibility that life will throw you a curveball. Try your best not to get caught up in the moment. Always be strategizing and you will be prepared for the good and the bad.

You can't allow anyone to stop your mission. Even if you hear people talk shit about you, you have to take that, *use* it, and execute. It's like a game of chess. Someone's mission is to take you out while you're playing the game, so you have to outthink them. You have to figure out what they're thinking and what your next move is going to be based on that—even if the person playing against you is *you*.

I'm not trying to *take dudes out*. I don't have any malicious intentions, but the point is, someone is going to end up giving you what you want, working with you, or on behalf of you.

Before you talked to them, they could never see themselves doing what you were asking. You have to outthink the other person.

If someone says anything malicious about you, you have to keep that in mind, know what they did and what they said. You have to remember if they were a part of shutting down any of your opportunities. Sometimes you've got to give up a little piece to get to a bigger piece. Sometimes you will take a hit and walk away with more than what you got hit for. You have to keep your eyes open to the big picture. Some people aren't worth cutting off because you can get something out of the situation before you decide to shut it down.

If you run into someone and you know they said some slick shit about you, try to act nonchalant. Even if you don't want to hang with someone, walk up to them, give them some love, and keep it moving. That can be considered fake or not real or playing a mind game—because why would you shake some-one's hand when you know what they said or the crap they were trying to pull behind your back?—but you will end up reaping the benefits. You just never know who people might be or who they are connected to.

I'm not about using people, and I want to make sure I'm clear on that. I don't sit around and tolerate a bunch of crap so I can use people. It's a fair exchange, no robbery. They have something I want and I have something they want. Even if they didn't think they wanted it, I am going to make them believe that they did, and it's going to happen.

You *cannot* be a pushover. You cannot be concerned that someone is thinking you're messed-up for not giving them what they're asking for. When you stay in that insecure space, you're going to give in to everybody and you won't be a master of your environment. Today, I am so comfortable in the way I feel. It took me a very long time to get here, but I just got more comfortable with telling people my truth. You cannot get self-conscious in your thinking. You can't worry about what other people are going to think about your speaking or thinking about *anything*, especially if you are on a mission to maximize your potential.

There is a time and a place for everything. You have to be selective about when you reveal how you may really feel about something, what you're thinking, and what you really want to say to someone. I tend to be very blunt about speaking my truth, and sometimes my timing can be off. When it is, I deal with the repercussions. Ultimately, you have to decide when to keep tight about the way you really feel about whatever is going on in your mind. You also have to know if the timing is right—and timing is everything. If the timing welcomes you to say exactly how you're feeling so you can create the best possible environment for you to be at your maximum potential, then go for it. Speak it, put it out there, and let people know.

I had to get to a level where I didn't give a shit. You have to get comfortable in your skin, just like plus-sized women would. I'm making that analogy here because it seems to me that plus-sized women are some of the most confident women out there and I have wondered how that is possible when society tells them they are "less than." She's heard every joke and seen every dirty look, but at some point, her mind-set changes and she thinks, *If I got through that, I can pretty much put up with anything that this world can dump in my lap.* She's experienced almost every human emotion that could ever be conjured up, but she ultimately steps into her own and knows that she's a great person, a beautiful person. In the same way, after a certain point you can step into your own, into a space of complete confidence, where everything is okay. It's not that you don't feel anymore, but you've become conditioned to it and you're fine with your reality. When you have dealt with all these different feelings and emotions over the years, you come to know your value and stand up for it.

A few years ago I found out people were screwing me over. I sharpened up, I found out what they did, and more important, I asked myself the questions, *What did I do? How was I carrying myself? What did I do to give these people the* permission *to do that to me?* I say to women, you can't expect men to treat you with respect or pay attention to your mind if your breasts and ass are hanging out and you look like a tramp. The same goes if someone is messing with you or treating you wrong. You have to find out what *you* decided for yourself. What were you doing to make people feel comfortable about taking advantage of you? Were you welcoming it? Maybe you were supposed to go through that so you could sharpen up and become better.

Originally, I was too trusting, especially with people who had a lot more experience and knowledge about certain business matters. People were giving me a lot of good energy, so I thought, *They must be good people. They must mean well by me.* When people have malicious intent toward you, they are using genuine moments of exchange and conversations to build that trust, all with the intention of screwing you over. If people are messing with you, you have to go back to yourself on that. You have to ask, like I did, *What about me or my personality and energy allowed them to be* comfortable *with screwing me?*

When I had my daughter, I felt as if my shirt *expanded*. At first I thought I could tolerate somebody messing with me a little bit, but I got *bold*. I started to live in my convictions. I am now living in my strength and my truth.

I run my business with the motto *Out of sight, out of mind*. This is pretty straightforward. You can't expect people to remember your name if you stay at home, away from the action. Unless you're running a home-based business, your chances for moving your career forward could be cut in half if you are not on people's radars. What you want to do can be increased by half if you just leave your house, get around the right people, and put yourself out there.

It all goes back to creating the mind-set of the people and building relationships. What do you want people to think of you? You can't assume that people think of you the way you think of yourself. You can change people's perceptions or views of you when you take more control of your identity. For example, if you're seen in a photo with a famous person and no one has ever heard of you a day in your life but it says "CEO of Such-and-Such with [that famous or successful person]," people may decide to Google you so they can find out who the other person in that photo is. People are very curious about what they see. Even the smallest exposure can create interest and make someone do a bit of research on you. If you're starting a business, you should have your website in place, so you can further what you're doing and gain more opportunities for connections and exposure.

You should *always be prepared*, because preparation meets opportunity. You should sit down and think of every possible scenario—from Facebook to Twitter to a website to T-shirts—branding and marketing that can help you further your business and create the mind-set of the people. Part of this preparation is preparing your spirit, because every level is another Devil. You need to strengthen your spirit to be ready for the opinions and put-downs you'll hear when people try to pull your plan apart. It seems to me that our president, Barack Obama, whom I have the most respect for, did his research and got prepared. He had a plan of attack for his campaign. With the very little that I know about politics, it seemed like he did so many fund-raisers and had so many foot soldiers across America, that he put himself ahead in the polls because he had so much money and all the right people endorsing his campaign. He had strategized and prepared his spirit and succeeded in creating the mind-set of the people.

Some people only associate relationships with celebrity and fame but that's not what it's about—it's about hustling and making any connection you can. Relationships work like this: If you go to party at a nightclub and the cover charge is thirty-five dollars, every person waiting out front to get into the club probably has thirty-five dollars in their pocket and then some. There are three hundred people in line waiting to get in, but if you have a *relationship* with the guy who works at the door, as soon as he sees you he's going to let you right into the club *and* he's going to let you bring your friends along. He's going to slap a wristband on you and escort you to the VIP section. That's how life works. The *relationship* you have with that man at the door is the reason you were able to bypass the three-hour wait. It's not about how much money you have or what you're capable of. It's about whom you know. A lot of you have been able to meet your favorite entertainer at some point. How much money did you have in your pocket? Were you famous? Most likely you didn't have a lot, and you weren't famous at all. But some way, somehow, a relationship enabled you to have that moment. The same thing goes for getting great seats or all-access backstage passes to a concert, restaurant reservations, advance copies of hot items, job interviews, important phone numbers, and anything that may help you enjoy yourself or get to the next level. It's the person you have a relationship and a connection with who gets you the access.

In general, whatever you're trying to do or get off the ground requires hustle. I am very impressed with people who understand the importance of hustling and they go all-out to do it just to reap the benefits in the end. You just have to be aware of everything, you have to be bold. Sometimes you have to wing it, take that leap of faith and discover.

Listening to God's Message

I've always had a relationship with God, and that's not going to change. But my prayers have changed. In the last five years or so, I have been thanking God for the blessings I've already received—everything that I am and everything that has happened and that I've been exposed to. I say these prayers more than the few prayers I say in which I ask for something that I really want or need.

I've learned to pray in silence so that I can hear God's response. There is power in silence. I believe that a lot of people are afraid of silence, peace, and serenity. When you pray and have a conversation with God, the spirit of someone else's opinion isn't welcome because the conversation you're having in that prayer is just between you and Him. I am in awe of the fact that God is receiving prayers from around the world in thousands of languages and that He takes the time to respond to me.

There is no right way to pray. People want and want and want, but I think we should pray for what we need and if we end up getting some of the stuff we want, that's just icing on the cake. So many people are struggling and going through tough times, and they're praying for their circumstances and their situation to change but they're not giving thanks for all the good things that already happened to them.

There's a song by Kim Burrell called "I Come to You More Than I Give," and it always moves me because she's saying that she asks God for more than she gives thanks for what she's already received. There's no right or wrong way to pray, but I believe paying our respects and recognizing that we've *already* been blessed opens up more opportunity for us to receive more of what we're asking for. We should stop praying for the wrong stuff—just asking for more and not giving thanks for what we've already received.

Everyone has their own relationship with God. I may not agree with all the dynamics. I always trip when people decide to bring God into situations, like into porn that I've seen in my day, or movies, or even in certain conversations. For example, in a movie, a woman is about to climax and says "Oh my God." Or someone may be about to rob a bank and they're praying that God keeps them safe before they commit a crime. Or they commit the crime and then pray constantly that they won't get caught. Or you see someone praying before they go in the ring to beat somebody's face in. There are a lot of very twisted relationships with God but, of course, to each his own.

My relationship with God is stronger when I'm in my darkest place. When I get really sad or bothered or am dealing with the loss of a friend or a family member that I really loved, or any difficult situation, God always appears in my darkest hour. He gives me a sense of direction without a map. I hear His voice and am uplifted with clarity from something that I didn't understand, or from something that I was going through. People associate God's favor with amazing things happening but I also think that God's favor helps you figure out things that you couldn't figure out on your own.

I believe that every lesson is a blessing, but we're not supposed to pray for drama. We're not supposed to pray for trials and tribulations to come our way just so we can *learn* from them.

People don't usually thank God for their problems while the problems are happening. When we are going through a tough time we don't associate it with God, we don't think of it as part of God's plan, that He's putting us through something so we can learn from it and come out better in the end. When people have problems they just try to survive. Only when it's all over do we start reflecting, thinking and *thanking*, and say *As bad as it was, thank God I was able to get through that.*

I would love to credit myself with all these things that have happened to me—all the different challenges and opportunities I've had—but it's all God. Jesus Christ in my life is the be-all and end-all to every aspect of everything that I am. Other than my child, I dedicate every aspect of my blessing and these opportunities that are created for me, to my relationship with Christ, and His having favor in my life. God had my life planned out and I'm just waking up every day discovering what He already had in mind for me.

God has blessed me with common sense and my common sense allows me to decide what's good for me or not. He is channeling Himself through me, and my common sense. All the ideas and concepts that I get excited about and the opportunities that present themselves are according to God's plan.

I don't believe in accidents. This may sound extreme, but if I get invited to an event, I will sometimes pray before I go to get some type of confirmation that an opportunity may present itself when I'm there. So that's why my blessings keep presenting themselves, because whether I'm going to a wild party or just having fun in itself, I believe I was supposed to be at that place, I was supposed to meet that person at that very moment at that very time, so that I can build a relationship or get on someone's radar about a project that we were supposed to do together—something they did or didn't have in mind for me, but that God had in mind for me. I can look at the bad stuff in this way, too: When I've made a mistake, I am able to see that in my positive mind-set as a lesson and *grow* from it.

People always say if you want to make God laugh, tell Him your plans. But sometimes God has something special in store for you, so you just have to *listen*.

Listen to your voice, listen to God's voice, and listen to your response. Try your best to have your response to God's message be according to God's message. Don't twist it or manipulate it. When God tells you to do something, do it. You can find yourself talking yourself out of doing certain things you know will be good for you—that's self-sabotage, self-defeat, you are standing in your own way. He is telling you what to do, He is telling you what not to do, He is telling you whom you should cut off, because you *think* the thought. As soon as you have second thoughts and think, *I shouldn't be in this, I shouldn't be doing this* and you figure out a way to talk yourself into doing it anyway, you may want to consider that you are technically ignoring your message.

The beautiful thing is, God gave us free will. When you are aware of what's right and what's wrong and you still decide to do wrong, that's because of your free will. It's your specific choice—you may not even consider what you're doing is wrong. The beauty of free will is that technically there is no wrong and there is no right—it's your opinion. There is a wrong and a right according to the Bible, but when it comes to free will, the definition of wrong falls into your individual opinion, unless you're living your life according to the word of God.

God is always there. He's with you throughout your choices, in the messages that He may have sent about which is the right choice, and through those choices you make through your own free will. He is with you through your bad choices and your good.

I'm not lazy in my relationship with God. I don't pray and just sit back and wait for His blessings or miracles and situations to come to pass. When I need to get motivated, I go to church and I talk to my pastor. When I'm making decisions— business and life decisions—and am struggling with an idea of what I should do, I go to church to get confirmation about a message God is sending me. There have been times I have gone to church and my pastor just happened to be talking about something pertaining to what I was trying to figure out. And that is my confirmation.

I pray, ask for guidance, and as I take the necessary steps, I ask Him to protect me and I pray for favor. More important, I execute. I could stay home and pray about it, which is just fine to some people, but that's not fine to me. You've got to pray *and* you've got to make up your mind that you're going to do something. You've got to get out there and do the work. That is when the blessings are revealed to you. I always say, *Don't be afraid of the unknown*. Just take that first step, take that leap of faith and with God you *will* land on your feet. Even if you fall you're going to somehow land on your feet, as long as you're moving and operating with God. Some people just need permission to be great. Some people need to recharge that battery in their back—the body just needs the jumper cables. You just need that spark and suddenly you can go out and make it happen.

In the midst of all the things I know and all the things I've been through, I know that God is using me to inspire others. Hopefully kids in the hood, teenagers, and men my age will look at me and think, *Tyrese did it, so I can do it*. I'm giving people permission to be better. God did it for me. Entertainers, entrepreneurs, and businessmen give people permission to be better when they're doing better.

I feel like God has put a real responsibility on my heart to put what I know out there into the universe. We shouldn't only associate giving back with cutting checks. God is love and love is God, so we should give back in whatever way we can. When I was younger, I wanted information on how to make my life better, and there are a lot of people out there who want the same. This is a lost generation. Everyone is desperate for information on how to better handle and deal with their circumstances. Everyone's desperate—even me. I flipped out when Will Smith dropped his knowledge on me because there were things that I didn't understand and he brought a level of clarity to my life in a way I just couldn't believe. The same thing happens with my pastor, Bishop Ulmer. Every Sunday when I go to church, it's like a therapy session—that's how powerful Bishop Ulmer's sermons are. He is a source of my fountain.

I hope you feel like I've given you permission to be great. Because I know you can be.

After reading this entire book you have the power to decide if this is just another book that you're reading and stay the same, or apply what you now know and change your life. I know a few people who have said that they've read hundreds and hundreds of books in their lifetime, but what do they do with the knowledge that they've gained? Don't be one of those people who read but don't make use of the information that they've come across. I do know that reading is a hobby for some, but I didn't write this book so it could be used as a relaxation device. Don't let it end up on your bookshelf.

At this point you can't say you don't know any better after reading this. There are some people who are content and happy with doing the same thing all of their life. Some people are happy and don't want anything else. Others want more and want options. What concerns me is when people have all this knowledge of self, and inspiration, and motivation and won't do anything with it. I hope you will apply and activate what you've read and that you'll get out of your own way and find your better place. I thank God for bringing you on this journey with me.

Acknowledgments

There are so many inspiring people who have impacted my life and been an extension of my backbone and a part of making me who I am today. I wanted to shout out a few people who helped me with this project:

Bishop Kenneth C. Ulmer: It's because of you that I feel closer to God and have grown closer to him and his word. You are the most articulate and passionate man of God I have ever been in the presence of. I can't put everything you mean to me into words. People can only hope that they come across a man that represents for the kingdom of God the way you do, so that they can be inspired to further their walk with God. Bishop, thank you from the bottom of my heart. I love you. You never know— one day I may just step up to that podium, and it will be *all* your fault for sure...

John Hope Bryant: A mentor isn't a mentor if what they speak falls on deaf ears...John, I love you and want you to know that after more than ten years not *only* am I still listening but I'm moving on what you make me aware of. I truly appreciate you and thank you for always being there.

Will Smith: One word comes to mind when I think of you: *selfless*. Being around your passion for life, knowledge, awareness, and heart has made me a better man all across the board. I feel not only lucky but honored to consider you a friend and more importantly a mentor who I know genuinely believes in me and wants the very *best* for me. I've said this to you before: After putting so much of myself out there it makes me uncomfortable at times to have it come back my way in the form of you having my best interest at heart. I can only say thank you.

Rev Run: Where do I start? You are a fearless man of God, a family man, and true friend of substance. You're an honest, sincere, and honorable man. I want to thank you not only for myself but for all of your millions of Twitter followers who are inspired by your daily messages. You have brought integrity and family values back to television and reminded us that "family" still exists in the world. I think it's great news for all of you, fans around the *world*, that Rev Run and I are penning our first book together, *Manology*. It's going to shake up the world!

Jerome Martin: From the beginning you have always been there and that story hasn't changed. You have became at this point more of a therapist and ear when I'm going through any and everything that life throws at me. You are a star. I love you and thank you for enduring this ride with me throughout all these years, first representing me at Ford Modeling agency and now as my personal A-List Hollywood agent...My life has been *transformed*—pun intended! Thank you, Jerome.

Isabella Castro, my "Queen of Execution": Everyone you interact with will agree that you are a force of nature. Your plate is so full—how is it possible for one woman to handle so much detail with such grace? I am screaming *thank you* and the people of the world echo that same feeling! There is so much more to do, so stay sharp! Love you!

Mike Le: Ten years and counting. What more can I say but that I love you and think you're the greatest! *K-Town*! E! Network, baby! What??? You are a true game changer.

Charles Austin aka Charlie Mack: It's rare to meet a man so consistent and grounded and *real*. Of all the people you know and love and who equally love you, I am very honored that you chose me to believe in and befriend. You have watched me grow like your own son and I believe we can both agree we have both made changes for the better. Thank you for always being the *best* version of you for the world. My hero!

Omar Shamout: Man, I can't wait to hit the road to announce to the world how all this got started. I thank you for being there from the embryo stage of this book. I know like me you're proud of where this started and how it turned out. You were there from the absolute beginning of the book and I can *only* thank you for believing!

Frank Weimann: My man Keenan Towns and I had a conversation about my passion to put out a book with all of my thoughts and inspiration and the first name he mentioned was yours. And now here we are with a book—wow! I want to thank you for believing and being a part of what the world is now going to experience.

Karen Thomas: You were our first stop in New York when we made our rounds to book publishers and the look in your eyes and your calming spirit while we were talking made me feel like Grand Central Publishing was my book's home. Thank you for being patient and fighting from the inside and staying on top of all things! Love you!

Gayle Atkins: Gayle, I love you. I just want to remind you that my career and everything is *all your fault*. Thank you for taking my call when I was only fourteen and believing in me and riding with me through it all. I love you forever!

Greg Parks: GPeeezy! Your name should be "Loyal for Life" because that's what you are. I got your back forever and that will *never* change.

Gerald Jackson: You are one of my best friends and have held me down for *ten yeaaars!* As my head of security you have a clean record—the only thing you didn't catch was that woman's high heel and I will forever hold a grudge...LMAO!! Love you man!

Reggie Andrews: I don't know where to start. I never knew what a father figure was till I met you. Every morning when I walked in that music class at Locke High School my life felt different because I was evolving and learning something new and you made it fun to learn. I *only* wish there was a class on "How to be the greatest teacher of all time" because you would for sure be the star of it! Mr. A, you are a brilliant man of integrity and I will forever love you. Blessings!

To my team of agents, lawyers, managers, and staff: It's damn near impossible to get to another level without having an incredible team in place and I can *only* thank you for everything you do from day to day. Let's keep plowing because the top is near. May God continue to bless my team.

Joelle Yudin: You are just too much to explain in words. Patient, patient, I repeat, patient. Only God knows how you were able to keep me focused to get this book done. You are a star writer, teacher, editor, and friend. Can you believe there are people around the world reading this? Surreal, right? Thank you Joelle. What a blessing it was to have you in my life to be apart of this process. We did it, baby! Cheers!

And to my daughter Shayla Gibson, my lovely, powerful, smart, and beautiful little girl: When you get older you're going to read and understand this. I always play a confidence game with you.

I ask you, *Who is the greatest?* Your response is *Shayla!* I say, *Who is the most powerful little girl in the world?* You say, *Shayla!* I ask, *Who is the smartest and most incredible little girl ever?* And you scream, *Shayla!* You are the best of me and your mother and I love you both with all my heart. Forever! I am so proud to be your father!

Every person on this list has in some way, shape, or form made me into the man that I am today. In this world one can only hope to come across someone who can help him along the way and have a genuine support system of powerful and inspirational people. I send my love to all of you. Even if you don't see your name on this list, know that you have contributed to my life and journey. I love you, too!

Akon, Lala and Carmelo Anthony, Avi Arad, Babyface, Anita Baker, Baker Winokur Ryder, Lorrie Barlett, T'shaun Barrett, Michael Bay, Michael Bento, Barris Bolton, AJ Brandenstein, Bill Braunstein, Ian Bryce, Kim Burrell, Lisa Callif, Dan Cardinali, Mike Case, Steve Cibulskis, Cheryl Coleman, Sean "Diddy" Combs, Communities in School (CIS) staff and students, Curtains, Karen Curry and family, Mayor Daley, Lee Daniels, George Daniels, Erick Dawkins, Julius Denem, Lorenzo Di Bonaventura, Vin Diesel, Tony Dixon, Josh Duhamel, Salendra Durham, Jason Edmonds, Tracy Edmonds, Derek Fisher, Herman Flores, Alan Foster, Darrell Foster, Brad Furman, Bill Furtkevic, Savon Gibson, Shonta Gibson, Tyrone Gibson Sr., Tyrone Gibson Jr., F. Gary Gray, Lyndsey Green, Shannon Hefferon, Taraji P. Henson, Deena Holland,

Howard University staff, Image Comics, International Creative Management, TD Jakes, Jeff Johnson, Andrew Jones, Quincy Jones, Juanita Jordan, Michael Jordan, Thuy-An Julien, Mark Kaplan, Todd Keith, R. Kelly, Gayle King, Robert Kirkman, David "GX" Kirkwood, Robert Kondrk, Karen Kosztolnyik, Kurupt, Shia LaBeouf, Linda Lau, Don Lee, Jacquie Lee, Jim Lee, Elva LeMasters, Daouda Leonard, Raymond Lewkow, Justin Lin, James Llewelyn, Nina Lugo, Ben Lyons, Anthony Mandler, Jillian Manus, Marcel Melanson, Harvey Mason, Brett Mayo, Kenny Meiselas, Jane Mentzinger, Todd McFarlene, Kate McGregor, Priscilla Murray, Brandy Norwood, President Barack Obama and Michelle Obama, Robert Offer, Linda Orel, Will Packer, Vicki Palmer, the Party City Team, Nicole Perna, Teddy Pendergrass—rest in heaven, Pendergrass family, Joe Puleio, Adriana and Omar Rambert, Brian Relyea, Dr. Sidney A. Ribeau, Garret Rittenberg, Gerry Rittenberg, Jeff Robinson, Kendra Robinson, Nancy Ryder, my dear Maya Saif, Brandon Salaam, Jill Scott, Ed Shapiro, Afeni Shakur, John Singleton, Richard Sledge, Snoop, Clinton Sparks, Steven Spielberg, T-Neal and the Core DJ Family, Tim Story, Joanetta Stowers, Jazmin Sullivan, Dwayne Swan, Brad Swart, Mark Tabb, Shakir Thomas, Darrell Thompson, Leon Timbo, Keenan Towns, Donald Trump, Iyanla Vanzant, Ron Waldman, Paul Walker, Tom Walper, Denzel Washington, David Webber, Marcus "Siege Monstrosity" White, Joanne Wiles, Oprah Winfrey, Elaine Wynn, Jordan Zimmerman, Zimmerman Agency, Robert Zuckerman. And to all my nieces, nephews, cousins, and extended family—I love you all.